INTERNATIONAL ARCHITECTURE & INTERIORS
Series directed by Matteo Vercelloni

LOFTS
&
APARTMENTS
IN NYC

MATTEO VERCELLONI
EDITED BY SILVIO SAN PIETRO
PHOTOGRAPHS BY PAUL WARCHOL

EDIZIONI
L'ARCHIVOLTO

IDEAZIONE E CURA DEL PROGETTO
Silvio San Pietro
Matteo Vercelloni

TESTI
Matteo Vercelloni

FOTOGRAFIE
Paul Warchol
Stephen Barker p. 11 (foto 10 e 16), p.138 (in alto), p. 139, p. 140

REDAZIONE
Matteo Vercelloni

PROGETTO GRAFICO COLLANA
Morozzi & Partners

PROGETTO GRAFICO LIBRO
Imago (Marina Moccheggiani, Francesca Giari)
Silvio San Pietro

REALIZZAZIONE GRAFICA E IMPAGINATO
Imago (Marina Moccheggiani, Francesca Giari)
Silvio San Pietro

TRADUZIONI
Daniela M. Brovedani

SI RINGRAZIANO
Gli architetti e gli studi di progettazione per la cortese collaborazione e per aver fornito i disegni dei loro archivi.
Si ringraziano inoltre tutti coloro che hanno reso possibile la realizzazione di questo volume, e in particolare
tutta la Fotolito San Patrignano e Imago.
We are grateful to the architects and designers who have kindly contributed to this project and have provided drawings
from their files.

[ISBN 88-7685-104-6]

© Copyright 1999
EDIZIONI L'ARCHIVOLTO
Via Marsala 3 - 20121 Milano
Tel. 02.29010424 - 02.29010444
Fax 02.29001942 - 02.6595552
e-mail: archivolto@homegate.it

I edizione novembre 1999

INDICE GENERALE
CONTENTS

PREFACE

This sixth volume in the series "International Architecture & Interiors" reflects on the theme of interior living environments, which was the subject of the first book. That first publication, printed a few years ago, gave rise to what has become a successful, precise and documented critical study of architectural environments made in the U.S.A. After only three years, this book, which is dedicated to a parallel analysis of the latest generation of lofts and some significant New York apartments, must be interpreted as a timely update of the more interesting design projects concerning interior environments. It also stands, however, as witness to the solutions and living styles, which, in recent years, have tended to emphasize the value of open spaces and of bright and spacious home environments that rely on new quality solutions, free of structural objects. The continuity between the first volume and the successive ones is also assured by the editorial choices, the sharpness and clarity of the layout and text and, of course, by Paul Warchol's photography. Page after page, his images guide the book's course, offering an impeccable and meticulous understanding of the various projects. He sensitively captures perspectives and pathways, colors and details, as well as the sense of space and the use of light, which is becoming increasingly more important even in domestic environments. The parallel meanings that until a few years ago defined loft and apartment as two distinct typologies, have now experienced some important changes and some blending of synergies.

The term loft, in its accepted meaning as a contemporary living style, originates in New York City. This is where, in the sixties, artists began taking over warehouses and factories in Soho and establishing their home-studios in them. Since then, the loft has become a sort of international household term used to refer to a large open-space, usually an industrial building, which is refurbished to accommodate activities that differ from those originally performed. Though lofts continue to be popular among painters and sculptors, lofts today house professional offices and private homes. This latest volume is dedicated to the latter category; that is, to lofts used as living spaces, to which small or midsize work areas are added. As well, the book examines a series of more traditional living areas, which can be compared to city apartments, though the loft is characterized by a stronger and more exclusive architectural structure.

Compared with the lofts of a few years ago, we noticed more attention is now given to the selection of overall architectural solutions. Primarily, they focus on the detail and creation of the compositional style. It appears that the loft, once considered an empty container, is now looked upon as an empty stage, to be 'filled' with new architectural figures and characterized by shapes and materials, pathways and internal perspectives. It is no longer seen as an industrial space, whose original dimensions must be respected. The variety of materials and the solutions used in creating today's lofts render them more like luxurious apartments, though, of course, the large, bright rooms find no comparison in traditional living environments. It is often difficult to imagine that only a few years ago these spaces were occupied by factories or warehouses. The lofts restructured by Tamara Baudec are an excellent example of this new living trend, her designs based on a certain demand of the real estate market, while the restructuring project carried out by ARCHITECTUREPROJECT, in the Flatiron quarter, is very refined. As well, Silvia Dainese's brilliant sensibility transformed a traditional New York loft, relying on memories of Italy to create the shapes and materials that characterize it. Some lofts, such as Diane Lewis', have added studios to their living spaces. LOT/EK also successfully restructured a loft for a professional couple, creating a home by using ready-made solutions.

So, while the loft becomes a living accommodation, characterized by an ample, multifunctional day area, the variety of layouts and compositions, which define many of the apartments, demonstrate a trend toward abandoning the traditional style of distinct rooms, located off a main corridor. While the day area and the night area are kept separate, guaranteeing the required privacy of the latter, the traditional dining room and kitchen, library and living room are now successfully blended within a single, unified space. This new style of combining living spaces into a single area is reminiscent of the traditional loft, characterized by its ample spaces. Benjamin Noriega-Ortiz's project, involving the residence of a fashion designer, exemplifies this new mode. The new layout features a central open-space area that extends across the entire length of the apartment, creating a succession of spaces. Another example is Gerner Kronick and Valcarel's interior design project in which the entire day zone is structured as a unified space along which the house's other rooms are placed, in a very dynamic manner. Lee Harvey Pomeroy's project is a symbolic and fascinating interplay between loft size and a knowledgeable and refined recreation of the classic New York apartment. The restructuring was based on one of the many monumental buildings in Central Park west, one of the longest standing symbols of the city's most exclusive residences. Another aspect of commonality between the two typologies of apartments that are represented in this book is the emphasis placed on the main structure of the living space. While the loft has always been characterized by tall iron, steel or cement columns, (see TRIARCH's or Morsa Studio's projects), the structure of city apartments has always been concealed by partition panels. The removal of these original partitions, which tends to open and enlarge the spaces of the day area, configuring the new layout solutions, has in some way forced the designers to emphasize the pillars and beams by highlighting their very shapes, construction materials and sizes. Such is the case for the apartment restructured by Stamberg & Aferiat, which overlooks the East River, or the refined urban residence designed by Gwathmey Siegel and planned in its every detail, beginning with the large structural cylinders that support the exposed ceiling beams. In addition to the careful attention given to the use of colors (Stamberg & Aferiat) and the use of different tonalities of light, which enable the internal ambience to be altered (Ken Kennedy in Midtown), the expositional aspect is also of paramount importance. In many apartments, this factor takes on a museum-like image. The owners of many of the apartments had requested that the solutions used in creating their living space also allow for a gallery, intended to display the art that they had acquired over the years. Pasanella, Klein Stolzmann and Berg were able to restructure two exclusive apartments, located on Central Park and Fifth Avenue, with rare sensibility. The result is a unified theme of images and comfort that characterizes these new urban homes, discreetly emphasizing and optimizing the precious art collections. Michael Gabellini, on the other hand, was inspired by the colors of the black and white photographs of the owner's collection. He was thus able to create a sequence of absolute spaces in the new apartment, which are emphasized by mahogany panels, strategically placed according to a well-orchestrated compositional structure. Instead, Parson Fernandez e Casteleiro's creativity and unstoppable experimental style defined the theme of symbolic triumph that inspired their work in the 'collector's home', an apartment that has become a sort of metaphorical museum that functions as a home. This traditional apartment was transformed, stripped of its traditional functions, allowing the sequence of its rooms to become a very symbolic exposition area.

Matteo Vercelloni

8

Con questo sesto volume della collana "International Architecture & Interiors", torniamo a riflettere sul tema degli interni domestici, oggetto del primo libro che qualche anno fa diede il via a quello che si è rivelato un progetto editoriale vincente, puntuale e documentata rassegna critica sugli ambienti dell'architettura made in Usa. A distanza di soli tre anni, questo libro, dedicato a un esame in parallelo dei loft dell'ultima generazione e di alcuni significativi appartamenti newyorkesi, deve essere inteso come tempestivo aggiornamento delle più interessanti esperienze progettuali dedicate agli spazi domestici, ma anche come testimonianza di nuove soluzioni e modi di abitare che tendono in questi ultimi anni a sottolineare il valore dello spazio libero, di luoghi per abitare luminosi e aperti, privi di vincoli funzionali e tesi verso nuove qualità ambientali. La continuità con il primo volume della collana, e con quelli successivi, è inoltre ribadita dalle scelte editoriali, dalla chiarezza d'impaginazione e di comunicazione e, ovviamente, dalle fotografie di Paul Warchol che scandiscono, pagina dopo pagina, il percorso del libro, offrendo una lettura impeccabile e rigorosa dei diversi progetti, cogliendo con sensibilità prospettive e percorsi, dettagli e colori, senso dello spazio e uso della luce, sempre più rilevante anche negli spazi abitativi. La lettura parallela tra loft e appartamenti ha evidenziato dei rilevanti slittamenti e delle sinergiche commistioni tra le due tipologie, che fino a qualche anno fa rimanevano distinte.

Il loft, nell'accezione data a questo termine dall'abitare contemporaneo, è immediatamente riconducibile alla città di New York, a quando negli anni Sessanta i primi artisti occupavano depositi e magazzini a Soho per stabilirvi i propri studi-abitazione. Da allora il loft è diventato una sorta di tipologia domestica internazionale, un termine impiegato per indicare un grande spazio unitario, in genere di tipo industriale, che viene riutilizzato per ospitare attività diverse da quelle originarie. Così se nei loft troviamo ancora studi di pittori e scultori, è facile vedervi anche studi professionali ed esclusive abitazioni. A quest'ultimo genere, il loft trasformato in particolare spazio domestico, molte volte affiancato anche da piccoli o medi spazi di lavoro, è dedicata la selezione proposta nel volume insieme a una serie di residenze più tradizionali, riconducibili alla tipologia dell'appartamento urbano, sia pure di tipo esclusivo e di forte carattere architettonico.

Rispetto ai loft degli anni passati notiamo una più approfondita ricerca della soluzione architettonica d'insieme, nell'attenzione rivolta alla cura del dettaglio e all'invenzione stilistico-compositiva. Sembra insomma che il loft, un tempo inteso come vuoto contenitore, sia assunto più come neutro palcoscenico da 'riempire' con nuove figure architettoniche e da caratterizzare per forme e materiali, percorsi e prospettive interne, piuttosto che come spazio industriale da mantenere nel rispetto delle dimensioni originarie. Per ricchezza materica e per soluzioni di progetto, i loft contemporanei si propongono in fondo come dei lussuosi appartamenti, certo con grandi e luminose stanze lontane dalle tradizionali dimensioni domestiche, e a volte diventa difficile pensare che sino a pochi anni fa questi interni erano occupati da attività artigianali o da magazzini. I loft ristrutturati da Tamara Baudec per essere immessi come nuove unità abitative sul mercato immobiliare, appaiono significative testimonianze di questa nuova tendenza, insieme al raffinato intervento di ARCHITECTUREPROJECT nel Flatiron District e a quello di Silvia Dainese che, nella trasformazione di un tradizionale loft newyorkese risolto con brillante sensibilità, ha saputo introdurre alcune memorie italiane a livello materico e figurativo. Alcuni loft, alla funzione di abitazione aggiungono quella di luogo di lavoro come quello che Diane Lewis ha ristrutturato per stabilirvi la propria casa e studio, o come l'intervento di LOT/EK, sorta di riuscito ready-made domestico per una coppia di giovani professionisti.

Così se il loft diventa un'abitazione caratterizzata da una vasta zona giorno multifunzionale, d'altro canto, molti degli appartamenti selezionati testimoniano nella loro varietà compositiva e differenza progettuale la tendenza ad abbandonare il consueto impianto a stanze separate con corridoio distributivo. Se viene sempre mantenuta la scansione tra zona giorno e zona notte, garantendo la necessaria privacy di quest'ultima, dall'altro le tradizionali sala da pranzo e cucina, biblioteca e soggiorno, si uniscono oggi in riuscite commistioni funzionali, all'interno di un unico grande spazio che proprio per le sue generose dimensioni ricorda le caratteristiche del loft. È il caso del progetto di Benjamin Noriega-Ortiz per la residenza di uno stilista di moda, dove un nuovo spazio centrale che attraversa l'intera lunghezza dell'appartamento organizza una significativa successione spaziale, o dell'esclusivo interno disegnato da Gerner Kronick e Valcarel dove l'intera zona giorno si pone come spazio unitario cui affiancare, in modo dinamico, le altre stanze della casa. Emblematico e affascinante per commistione tra la dimensione del loft e quella di una sapiente e raffinata rivisitazione del classico appartamento newyorkese, appare l'intervento di Lee Harris Pomeroy in uno degli edifici monumentali di Central Park West, da sempre luogo simbolo delle residenze più esclusive della città. Un altro aspetto comune alle due categorie domestiche oggetto del libro, presente in gran parte dei progetti selezionati, è la messa in luce della struttura portante dell'abitazione. Se nei loft le alte colonne in ghisa o in ferro, ma anche in muratura, sono sempre state il segno distintivo con cui confrontarsi (vedi i progetti di TRIARCH e dello Studio Morsa), negli appartamenti urbani la struttura era sempre nascosta dai tavolati divisori e dai loro incastri. La demolizione di divisioni preesistenti, tendente ad aprire e ad ampliare gli spazi della zona giorno, configurando nuove soluzione planimetriche, ha in un certo modo costretto i progettisti a evidenziare pilastri e travi enfatizzandone a volte la figura per trattamento materico e volume, come nell'appartamento affacciato sull'East River firmato da Stamberg & Aferiat; o nella raffinata residenza urbana, disegnata in ogni dettaglio da Gwathmey Siegel, da cui emergono forti cilindri strutturali a sostegno delle travi a vista del soffitto. Insieme all'attenzione verso l'impiego del colore (Stamberg & Aferiat) e all'uso della luce a diverse tonalità, in grado di cambiare l'atmosfera d'interni (Ken Kennedy a Midtown), di grande interesse appare anche l'aspetto espositivo, quasi museale, che troviamo in alcuni appartamenti. In alcuni casi una delle richieste espresse dalla committenza era quella di organizzare l'esposizione delle diverse collezioni d'arte raccolte nel tempo. Pasanella, Klein Stolzmann e Berg hanno affrontato con rara sensibilità in due esclusivi appartamenti affacciati su Central Park e Fith Avenue, il tema di unire all'immagine e al comfort di due nuove residenze urbane l'attenzione verso una valorizzazione discreta e non incombente di preziose collezioni d'arte. Michael Gabellini ha invece preso spunto dalle tonalità della raccolta di fotografie in bianco e nero del suo committente, per organizzare la sequenza di spazi assoluti del nuovo appartamento, scandito da setti in mogano disposti secondo una calibrata regia compositiva. Il trionfo simbolico, materico e figurativo della 'casa del collezionista', sorta di metafora museale tradotta in chiave domestica, è invece il tema di progetto sviluppato con grande creatività e irrefrenabile sperimentazione, da Parson Fernandez e Casteleiro in un tradizionale appartamento che ha dimenticato le proprie funzioni tradizionali per trasformare la sequenza delle proprie stanze in luoghi espositivi dal forte valore simbolico.

Matteo Vercelloni

9

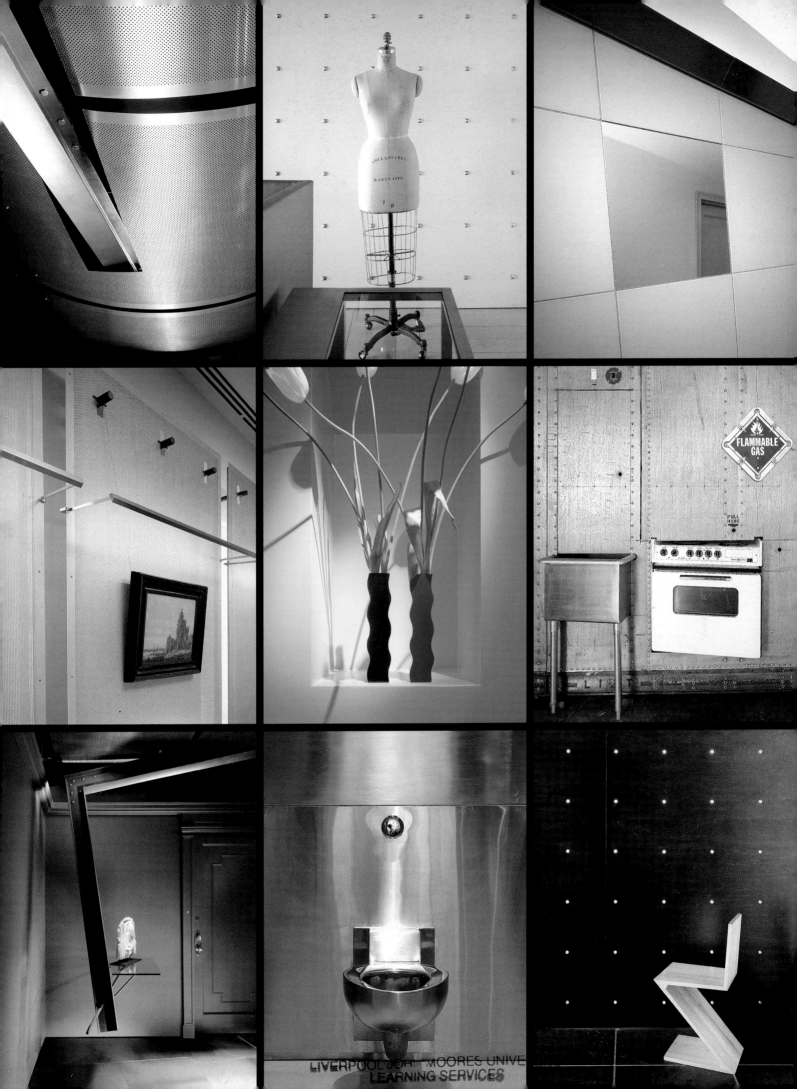

LIVERPOOL JOHN MOORES UNIVERSITY
LEARNING SERVICES

RIGORE CROMATICO
CHROMATIC RIGOR
ARCHITECTUREPROJECT LLP, 1998

This spacious loft in the Flatiron district was completely restructured in order to create a new living space, which could be used as both, a home and an office. Its uses were meant to be extended to business dinners and luncheons, as well as meetings. The owner, a professional who works in the public relations field, wanted an interior design that would also enable him to expose his contemporary art collection in the best possible manner. The designers, therefore, planned the entire project around a range of colors inspired by the paintings of Brice Marden. Little remains of the loft's original industrial aspect. There is only the reminder of a unified space joined by the parts that make up the entrance/dining room/living room/study, built on various levels. This series of spaces constitutes the public area of the house, where the color pallet has left a definite and calibrated mark. Vertically painted colors characterize some of the walls, which, like those between the living room and the studio, have also been separated from the ceiling. Horizontally, the oak floors provide a harmonious color match. The same tones are, in fact, used in the parquet, transforming it into a prominent element of composition. Ceilings, cylindrical pillars and most of the walls have been painted white, thereby emphasizing the chromatic episodes. The private living space, located behind the exhibition gallery in front of the entrance, has been placed along the lateral façade, permitting the creation of two large bedrooms with bathrooms and independent closets. A dark blue curve marks the wall that leads to the kitchen, providing a very scenic entry. The kitchen is located in an irregular area next to the main entrance, where it is very discreetly connected to the dining room. The furniture, a blend of tailored designs and classical pieces selected from the Modern Movement (Mies van der Rohe, Arne Jacobsen), also follow the color scheme, highlighting the carefully studied choices and rigorous chromatic patterns of the ensemble.

Questo spazioso loft nel Flatiron District è stato oggetto di una completa ristrutturazione per definire un nuovo spazio domestico in grado di funzionare sia come confortevole abitazione, sia come luogo di lavoro per accogliere pranzi e cene, riunioni e incontri. Il proprietario, un professionista impegnato nel campo delle pubbliche relazioni, chiedeva di pensare alla nuova architettura d'interni anche dal punto di vista espositivo, per ospitare nel migliore dei modi la propria collezione d'arte contemporanea. A questa componente si sono riferiti i progettisti, che hanno caratterizzato l'intero progetto intorno a una gamma di colori ispirati alla pittura di Brice Marden. Il rigore delle scelte cromatiche, scandite dalla serie grigio/blu-marrone-cioccolato/blu scuro, è stato assunto come strumento di connessione tra gli elementi fissi e gli oggetti del progetto, tra scelte architettoniche e arredi. Dell'aspetto industriale originario, il loft mantiene solo il ricordo di spazio unitario costituito dall'articolato insieme dell'ingresso/sala da pranzo/soggiorno/studio, giocato su differenti livelli. Questa serie di spazi costituisce la zona pubblica della casa, dove la palette cromatica emerge con decisa e calibrata regia sia nell'uso verticale, per caratterizzare alcune pareti e quinte staccate dal soffitto come quella tra soggiorno e studio, sia per le componenti orizzontali costituite dal pavimento in rovere. Le stesse tonalità vengono, infatti, impiegate per colorare il parquet trasformandolo in elemento compositivo rilevante. Soffitti, pilastri cilindrici e gran parte delle pareti sono stati verniciati di bianco, valorizzando così gli episodi cromatici. La zona privata dell'abitazione, organizzata alle spalle della galleria espositiva di fronte all'ingresso, è stata ubicata lungo la facciata laterale ricavando due ampie camere da letto con bagni e cabine armadio indipendenti. La cucina, anticipata da una parete in curva blu scuro di effetto scenografico, occupa invece una zona irregolare a fianco dell'ingresso ed è collegata in modo discreto alla sala da pranzo. Anche gli arredi, alcuni su disegno altri selezionati tra i classici del Movimento Moderno (Mies van der Rohe, Arne Jacobsen), seguono le tonalità della palette di riferimento, sottolineando lo studiato rigore cromatico d'insieme.

13

14

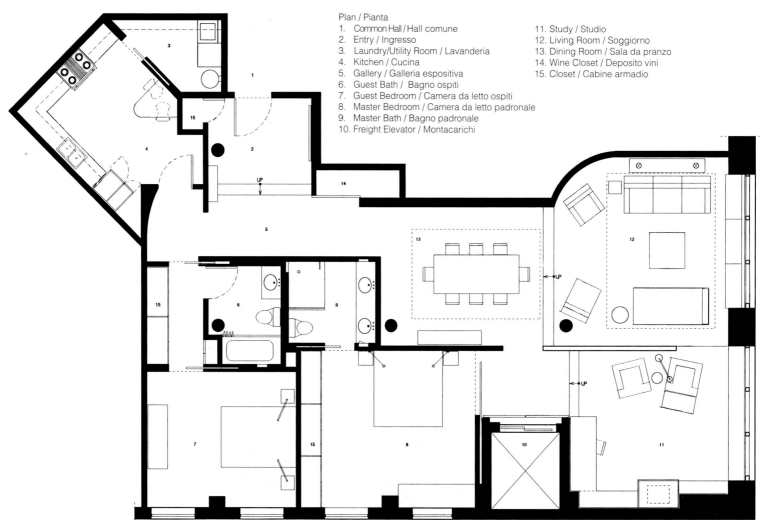

Plan / Pianta
1. Common Hall / Hall comune
2. Entry / Ingresso
3. Laundry/Utility Room / Lavanderia
4. Kitchen / Cucina
5. Gallery / Galleria espositiva
6. Guest Bath / Bagno ospiti
7. Guest Bedroom / Camera da letto ospiti
8. Master Bedroom / Camera da letto padronale
9. Master Bath / Bagno padronale
10. Freight Elevator / Montacarichi

11. Study / Studio
12. Living Room / Soggiorno
13. Dining Room / Sala da pranzo
14. Wine Closet / Deposito vini
15. Closet / Cabine armadio

ADAM FUSS

JAPANESE ART AFTER 1945 SCREAM AGAINST THE SKY

ALEXANDRA MUNROE ABRAMS

NOW BECOMING THEN DUANE MICHALS

TRIBECA LOFT

Tamara Beudec Architect + atelier, 1997

This loft, which is located in the Tribeca quarter, was part of a project that involved the complete restructuring of artisan-storage workshops, as well as a series of superimposed living units. Since the lofts were specifically designed to be sold, they are, therefore, projected as neutral open-space areas. The walls have been painted white, while the pavements are covered in wooden girders, which, in some way, are reminiscent of their industrial past. The incompleteness of these open-spaces was intended to allow the creative imaginations of its future inhabitants to be fulfilled. Despite the lack of a future user and, hence, of a specific request regarding the interior decor, the proposed solution is very convincing. As the designer herself confirms, the "complete incompleteness" has been the challenge of this restructuring project. The spaces are long and narrow, in some cases, extending across the entire length of the block, providing a view on both, the North and South sides. The original plan presented only two significant windows along the narrow ends, influencing the final layout decisions to place the day areas along this façade. Consequently, the kitchen opens onto the open-space living room and dining room, while the new fireplaces were built into the blind walls. The latter are a fundamental element of the new layout. The elevator and stairway were centrally located so that they would service both lofts. From the entrance, the lofts access a study-bedroom, which is immediately followed by a large space in which two bathrooms, a laundry room and a closet have been ensconced. The construction of this space, a sort of niche, which houses the domestic commodities demanded by the market, has actually become the focal point of the architectural design. The walls that delineate this space are of varying heights and they are disconnected from the ceiling, thereby maintaining the unified characteristic of the loft. The bathrooms are the sole exception to this. By necessity, the walls of these rooms are connected to the ceiling, creating a series of thin, horizontal glass partitions which, when they are lit from the interior, provide a very particular and scenic effect that blends perfectly with the Big Apple's skyline.

Il progetto di questi due loft, ricavati all'interno di un edificio industriale nella zona di Tribeca, è parte della generale conversione del fabbricato da laboratori artigianali-depositi a

Plan / Pianta

serie di unità abitative sovrapposte, interamente ristrutturate. I loft ristrutturati sono stati progettati per essere messi sul mercato; anche per questo si presentano come spazi neutri, dalle pareti bianche e con un pavimento a doghe di legno che in qualche modo ricorda il passato industriale dell'edificio. Spazi che denunciano la loro incompletezza proprio come grado di libertà lasciato volutamente a chi vi abiterà. Tuttavia, nonostante l'assenza di un diretto fruitore e quindi la mancanza di richieste, la soluzione proposta appare più

che convincente. Come afferma la progettista, la "completa incompletezza" è stata la vera sfida nella ridefinizione di questi spazi. Di forma stretta e allungata, con dimensioni in grado di attraversare l'isolato e affacciarsi su una via a Sud e un'altra a Nord, l'edificio a pianta libera presentava due sole significative aperture lungo le strette testate. Questa oggettiva morfologia ha indirizzato le scelte compositive a disporre lungo le facciate le zone giorno caratterizzate dalle cucine aperte verso gli spazi unitari soggiorno-pranzo e da nuovi essenziali camini ricavati lungo il muro cieco. Il blocco scala-ascensore è stato ricavato in posizione centrale all'edificio per servire entrambi i loft. Questi trovano nella zona dell'ingresso, subito dopo il locale studio-camera da letto, uno studiato incastro volumetrico dove sono disposti due bagni, la lavanderia e una cabina armadio, spazi domestici richiesti dalle esigenze e dalle strategie di mercato. La costruzione di questo funzionale nocciolo-servizi delle nuove unità abitative è diventato anche il fulcro architettonico che ne caratterizza lo spazio. I muri che definiscono l'incastro volumetrico hanno diversa altezza e non raggiungono il soffitto ad eccezione dei bagni, conservando così il carattere unitario del loft. Le pareti dei bagni, necessariamente connesse al soffitto, presentano una serie di strette vetrate orizzontali che nelle ore serali, a luci interne accese, danno al blocco architettonico un riuscito effetto scenografico che ben si rapporta allo skyline della Grande Mela.

Loft B

Loft B

Loft B

Studies on lighting / Studi per la luce

Loft A

Loft A

STRUTTURA A VISTA
EXPOSED STRUCTURE
Silvia Dainese Architect, 1995

Once used as a warehouse, this traditional New York loft, with windows located on a single façade overlooking the vast, tree-lined Ericson Place in the Tribeca district, has now been transformed into a refined and exclusive living accommodation. Full advantage has been taken of the natural light that enters this fifth-floor loft from its original windows on the west wall. The bordering area, assigned to a parking lot, made the addition of another seven windows possible, since construction was not permitted on this end. This important alteration allowed for the creation of two walls of windows, as well as the opportunity to optimize the new internal spaces by completely separating the ample open-space living room from the bedroom. The owner's need for large spaces in which to entertain friends and guests, coupled with the need to have a more private, if contained, living space, was brilliantly resolved by placing the living room with fireplace and piano along the wall facing the piazza. The American-style kitchen overlooks this area, functioning as a fixed furnishing and providing an important domestic flare. It is comprised of neatly designed alterations between wood surfaces and Carrara marbles. Next to the kitchen, the master bedroom is accessed via a mosaic door on visible steel runners, which also serves as a sort of large decorative panel. Coupled with the majolica that are encased in the floor in front of the fireplace, these elements stand as a reminder of the owner's Italian origins. The ample living room was created from the original available space, using the cast iron colonnade that supports the longitudinal beam, made of the same material, upon which the rafters of the restored wooden floor have been laid. The exposed structure, which crosses the entire length of the loft, becomes the focal point of the new layout, strongly determining the essence of the hallway-entrance and guiding the view into the living room. This view is framed by the opening created by the revolved kitchen space. The concave bookshelves respond to the compositional technique used to transfer the kitchen space. Their external protrusion hides a sauna in their interior, efficiently separating the entrance from the living room.

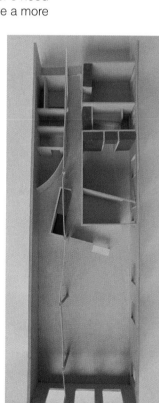

Un tradizionale loft newyorkese, impiegato un tempo come magazzino, con un solo fronte finestrato affacciato sull'ampia sistemazione alberata di Ericson Place nel quartiere di Tribeca, è stato trasformato in una raffinata ed esclusiva abitazione. Lo spazio interessato dall'intervento, ubicato al quinto piano, sfrutta al meglio la luce proveniente dalle aperture originarie cui si sono aggiunte ben sette nuove finestre lungo il lato ovest, passibile d'intervento grazie all'area limitrofa resa non edificabile e adibita a parcheggio. Questo rilevante cambiamento ha permesso di avere due lati finestrati e di ottimizzare la nuova disposizione interna, separando nettamente l'ampio soggiorno open space dalla zona notte. Le esigenze del committente, di ampi spazi per ricevere amici e ospiti, ma anche di una zona più privata con dimensioni raccolte, sono state risolte in modo brillante, organizzando lungo il fronte sulla piazza il soggiorno con camino e pianoforte, su cui si affaccia la cucina all'americana. Questa è pensata come arredo fisso e segno domestico di riferimento, composta da studiati incastri tra superfici di legno e marmo di Carrara. Di fianco al complesso mobile cucina si accede alla camera da letto padronale, annunciata da una porta in mosaico, scorrevole su binario di acciaio a vista, proposta anche come sorta di grande pannello decorativo che, insieme alle maioliche incassate a pavimento di fronte alla bocca del camino, ricordano l'origine italiana della progettista. Nell'ampio soggiorno emerge l'uso della significativa struttura originaria con colonnato in ghisa di sostegno per la lunga trave longitudinale dello stesso materiale, su cui poggiano i travetti del solaio di legno restaurati. La struttura a vista, che attraversa tutto lo spazio del loft, diviene l'elemento di riferimento per la nuova disposizione planimetrica segnando fortemente l'andamento del corridoio-ingresso e la prospettiva interna verso il soggiorno. Questa è incorniciata dall'apertura ottenuta nel blocco ruotato della cucina. A questa significativa traslazione volumetrica, risponde a livello compositivo la libreria in curva prospiciente, un mobile su disegno che, nascondendo la sauna al suo interno, crea un efficace spazio distributivo d'ingresso al soggiorno.

26

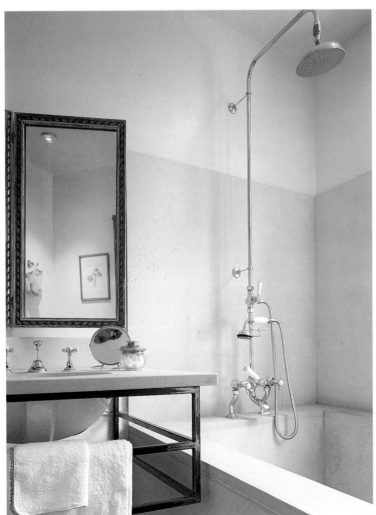

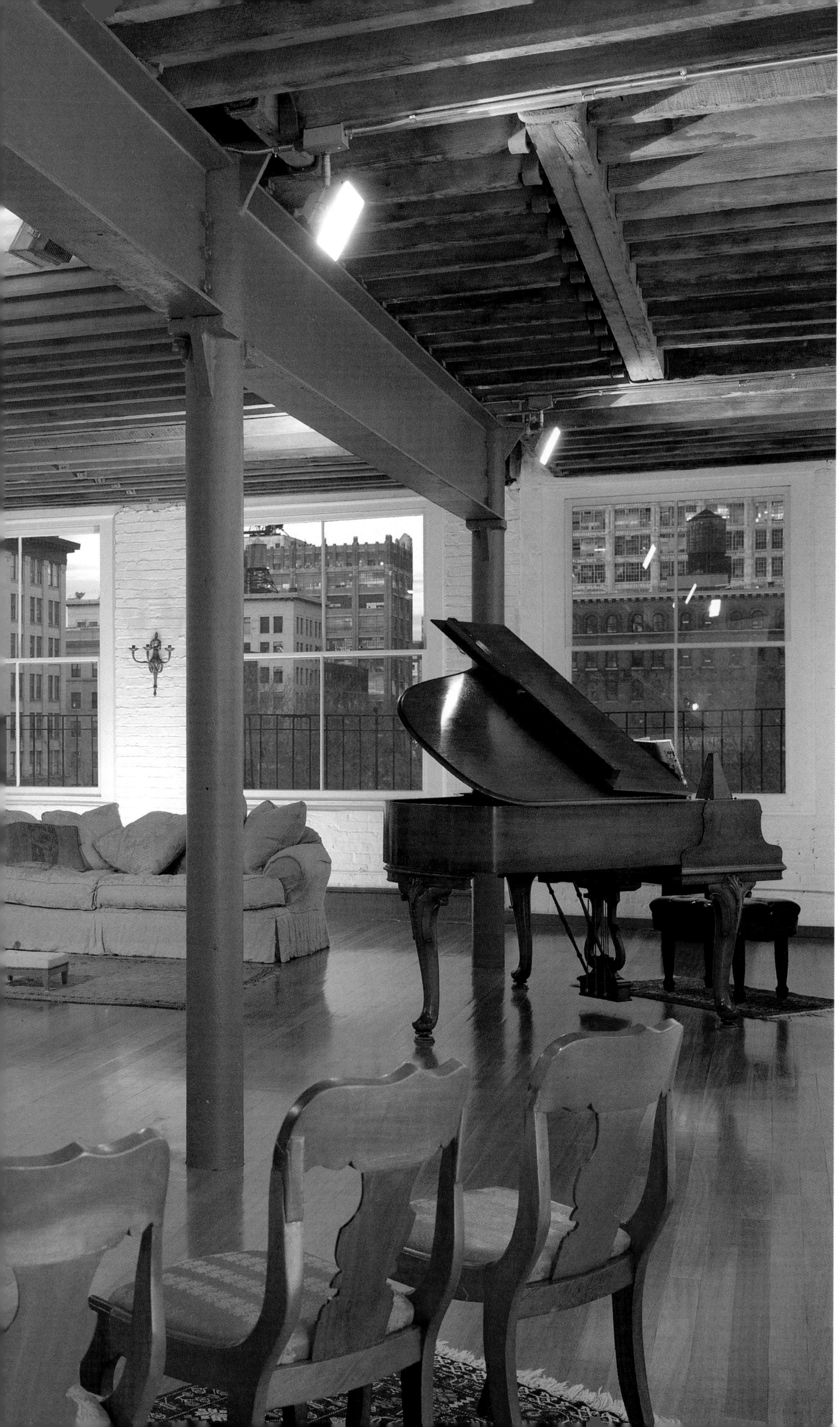

FIXED SCENE

Winka Dubbeldam Archi-TECTONICS, 1998

This fifth-floor loft, characterized by a traditional central colonnade, was part of a restructuring project in Soho. Unlike other such buildings, the five columns and support beams were in solid wood and they were kept as principal and significant reference points. The project's solution emphasized a change in both, space and size. The night area and the small library were placed behind and beside a sculpted wall made of steel panels supported by glazed glass panes, often used as doors. The result is an architecturally striking scene staged in the ample day area, where several compositional elements were blended, enhancing the luminous open-space. The bathroom separates the library and the bedroom, presenting a domestic image of the house, thanks, in part to the use of the wood that covers the floors and some of the walls. Immense curtains and custom-made furniture complete the effect, especially in the master bathroom, where steel was used to cover most of the surfaces. A gray-blue, full-height velvet curtain separates the bedroom from the glassed area and the day zone. A fireplace with a lateral opening enhances the image. In the immense day area, where the original layout of the open-space loft has been preserved, the series of wood columns is emphasized by the presence of a long breakfast table with a double surface, which has been bolted to the cylindrical trunk. The raised surface was also designed to highlight the kitchen, created in steel, drawing attention to the hallway that leads to the service areas. The separate, closed space between the kitchen and the night zone houses a guest bathroom, created using an effective blend of materials, plastic and embeddings, forming a marked geometrical pattern. The living and dining rooms, located along the main façade, characterized by its arched windows, are flanked by a terrace. A glass roof reflects the shapes and materials of the interior spaces, protecting the latter.

32

Nel quartiere di Soho è stato ristrutturato questo ampio loft ubicato al quinto piano di un tipico edificio a pianta libera, segnato dal tradizionale colonnato centrale. A differenza di altri edifici simili, le cinque colonne e la trave sostenuta si presentavano di legno massiccio e sono state assunte come forte ed oggettiva preesistenza di riferimento. La soluzione progettuale ha portato all'interno del loft una precisa scansione volumetrica e spaziale: la zona notte e una piccola biblioteca sono organizzate alle spalle e a fianco di una movimentata parete scultorea composta da profilati di acciaio a sostegno di superfici in vetro acidato impiegate a volte come porte a lastra continua; una riuscita e studiata scena fissa che si propone come conclusione scenografica e architettonica dell'ampio spazio della zona giorno dove si sommano diverse funzioni all'interno dell'unico luminoso spazio. La biblioteca, le camere da letto e il bagno tra loro frapposto, esprimono una dimensione fortemente domestica e raccolta, con pavimenti e alcune delle pareti di legno, ampi tendaggi e riusciti arredi su disegno tra cui l'intero bagno padronale pensato come raffinata scatola architettonica rivestita in parte di acciaio. Una tenda di velluto grigio-azzurra a tutt'altezza separa dal volume vetrato e dalla zona giorno la camera da letto padronale, arricchita da un caminetto scultoreo con bocca laterale. Nel grande spazio della zona giorno, dove è ricordato il carattere unitario del loft preesistente, la successione delle colonne lignee è sottolineata da un lungo tavolo per il breakfast, con doppio piano, fissato con una staffa imbullonata al fusto cilindrico. La doppia superficie a sbalzo è stata disegnata anche per delimitare la zona della cucina di acciaio posta lungo la parete alle sue spalle che scandisce il corridoio di distribuzione agli spazi di servizio. Tra cucina e zona notte è stato costruito un volume chiuso dove è stato ricavato il bagno degli ospiti disegnato come riuscito spazio plastico, frutto di governati incastri e di rigorosi giochi geometrici. Lungo la facciata principale, segnata dalle finestre ad arco, sono disposti soggiorno e zona pranzo, affiancati da una terrazza protetta con una pensilina di vetro che riprende figure e materiali della scena fissa dell'interno.

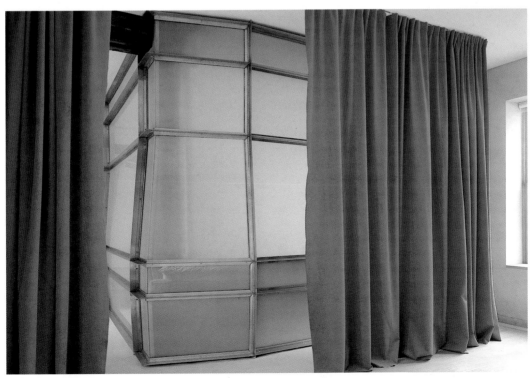

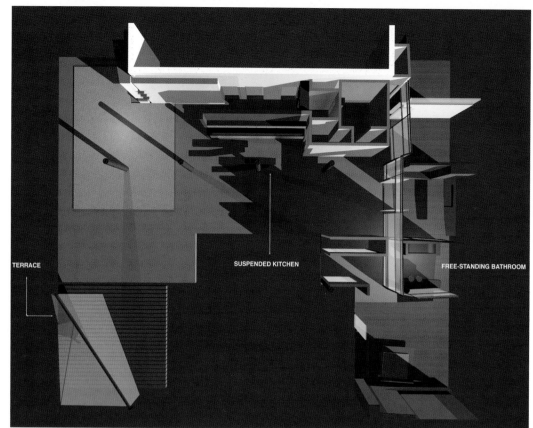

TERRACE   SUSPENDED KITCHEN   FREE-STANDING BATHROOM

Perspective from top / Prospettiva dall'alto

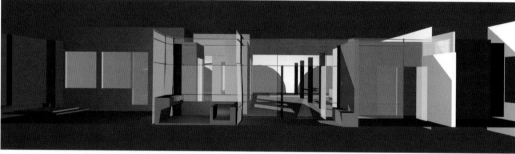

Longitudinal section / Sezione longitudinale

Living room perspective / Prospettiva del soggiorno

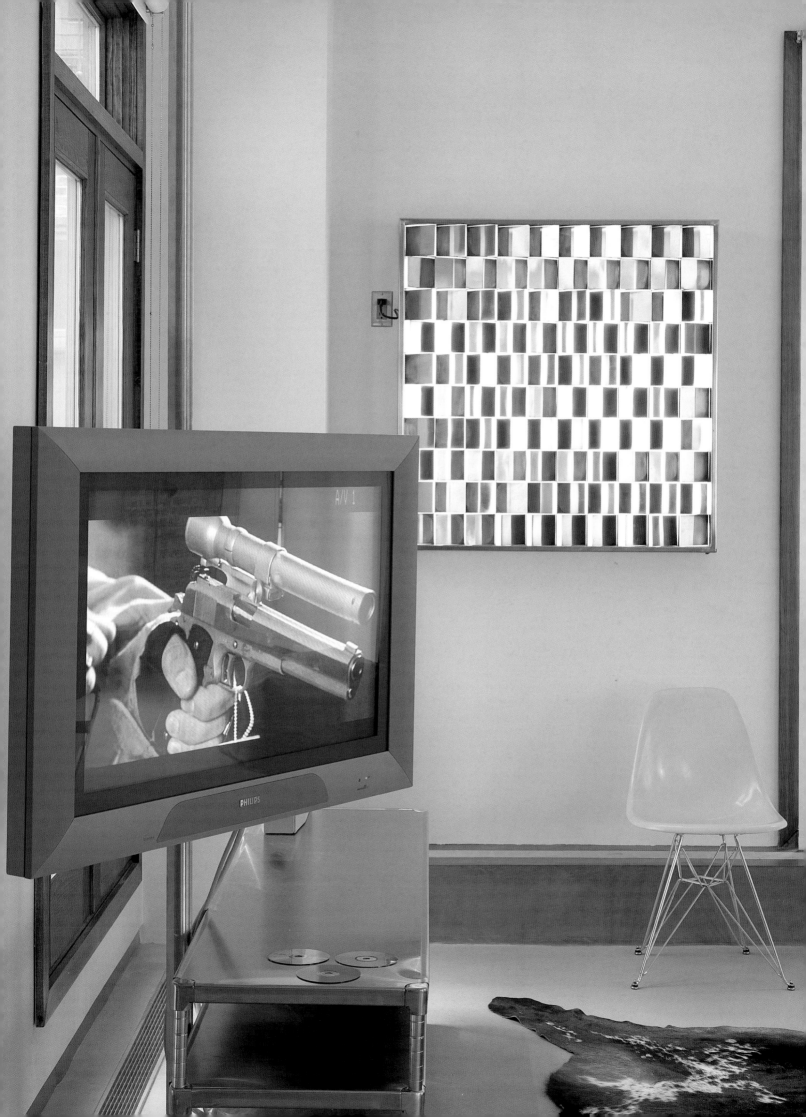

DOMESTIC SCENES
Karen Fairbanks-Scott Marble Architects, 1997

The loft inside this building was restructured to create a unique living space for a choreographer. The project's design was inspired by the world of theatre and show business, and its relative stage mechanisms. The focal point of composition was born of the stage's use of sliding curtains, which, like those used in stage productions, have been designed in a variety of shapes and fabrics. Since the L-shaped space presented a series of windows along a single side of the structure, a large portion of available space was poorly lit. Additionally, it proved complicated to divide the space without worsening the existing lack of natural light; hence, the master bedroom was placed against the windowed façade, along with the living room/dining room. The poorly lit area of the entry was optimized by creating a space that could be altered by using glass panels or furniture. From here, the kitchen opens onto the living room. The room next to the kitchen can be used as either an extension of the dining room or as a guest bedroom with private bath, which was built next to the entry along with a storage area located behind the kitchen. A sliding, perforated steel panel allows the guest room to be separated from the kitchen, when needed. The steel screen can extend as far as the sandblasted glass panel of the guest bathroom, covering it, thereby isolating the guest area completely. In this way it becomes a successful element of reference. The two areas of the loft are further delineated by their flooring. In the brighter section of the loft, a cherry wood parquet has been used, while a slate pavement completes the entry and guest bathroom. Cork has been used in the guest room and in the kitchen. The kitchen furniture complements the sliding panel as it, too, is made of steel. Though the work table has a shelf made in cork, the part facing the living room has been made in cherry wood to match the parquet. An acidified glass panel, supported by a thin, black metallic border and a Venetian curtain with colored listels separate the living room from the bedroom. The latter is equipped with a walk-in closet. Another glass panel is used as a sliding door, accessing the master bath, which is covered in a light blue glass mosaic.

All'interno di un edificio è stato ristrutturato questo loft per ricavarne l' abitazione di una coreografa. Al mondo del teatro, dello spettacolo e dei meccanismi del palcoscenico sembra in fondo rifarsi la ricercata soluzione progettuale che ha trovato come spunto compositivo l'idea delle quinte scorrevoli, di diversa figura e materiale, proprie delle scenografie teatrali. Lo spazio disponibile, con pianta a 'L', presentava una serie di aperture lungo un solo lato. Di conseguenza gran parte dell'ambiente era poco illuminato e difficilmente divisibile senza peggiorare ulteriormente l'oggettiva assenza di luce naturale. La scelta compositiva e distributiva ha posto

lungo il fronte finestrato la camera da letto padronale e il soggiorno-pranzo. La zona meno illuminata dell'ingresso è stata invece sfruttata per creare un ambiente trasformabile con pareti vetrate o mobili. Qui la cucina, aperta sul soggiorno, è affiancata da una stanza che può essere usata secondo le esigenze come ampliamento della zona pranzo o come camera degli ospiti con bagno indipendente, ricavato di fianco all'ingresso insieme a un locale deposito alle spalle della cucina. Una quinta scorrevole di acciaio, forata secondo una maglia ortogonale, permette di separare o unire la stanza degli ospiti alla cucina. Lo schermo di acciaio può estendersi sino a coprire la lastra di vetro sabbiato del bagno di servizio separando così completamente la zona ospiti, proponendosi come elemento compiuto di riferimento.
Le due zone del loft sono caratterizzate anche da una diversa pavimentazione: parquet di ciliegio per la parte più luminosa, ardesia per ingresso e bagno di servizio, sughero per camera ospiti e cucina. L'acciaio della parete scorrevole trova nei mobili della cucina dello stesso materiale un elemento complementare. Il banco di lavoro con piano in ardesia presenta invece verso il soggiorno un fronte di legno di ciliegio, per raccordarsi al parquet prospiciente. Una quinta in vetro acidato, sostenuta da un sottile profilato metallico nero, separa, insieme a una tenda veneziana in listelli cromati, il soggiorno dalla camera da letto, fornita di una cabina armadio passante. Un'ulteriore lastra vetrata è impiegata come porta scorrevole per accedere al bagno padronale, rivestito in mosaico di vetro azzurro.

43

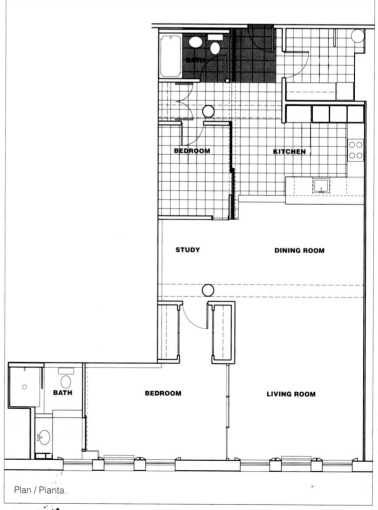

BATH

BEDROOM   KITCHEN

STUDY   DINING ROOM

BATH   BEDROOM   LIVING ROOM

Plan / Pianta.

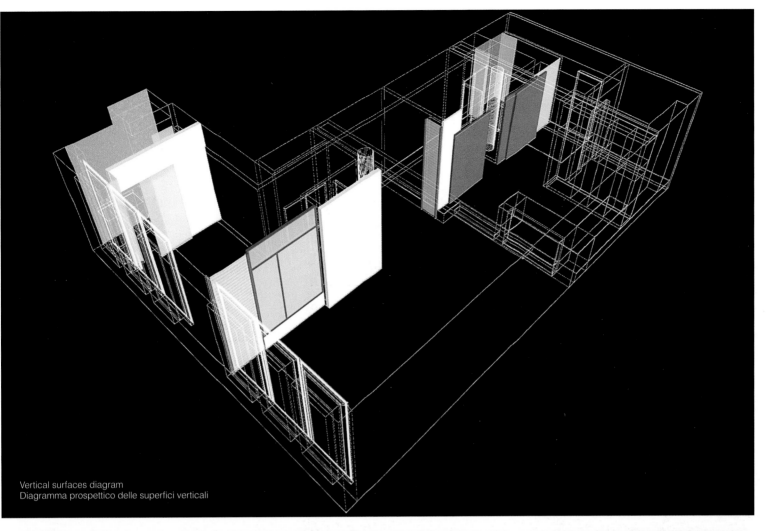

Vertical surfaces diagram
Diagramma prospettico delle superfici verticali

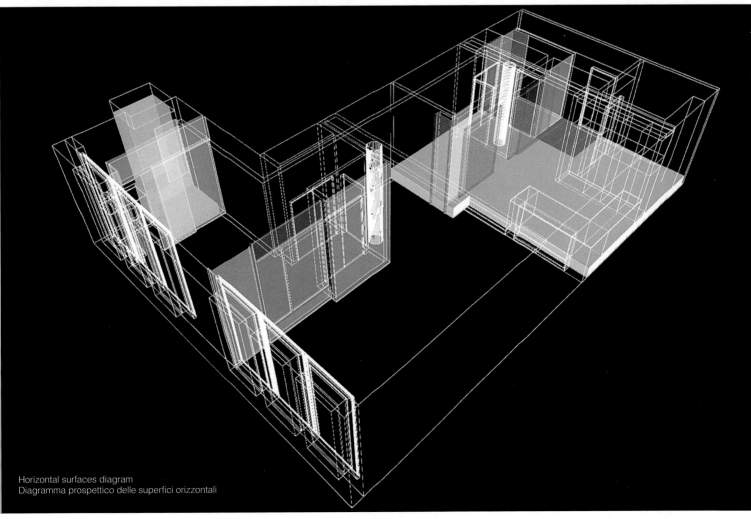

Horizontal surfaces diagram
Diagramma prospettico delle superfici orizzontali

AUTOCOSTRUZIONE
SELF-CONSTRUCTION
Paul Henderson / Beth Sigler Architects, 1998

On the last floor of an industrial building in Queen's, an open-space laboratory, equipped with a windowed double façade, was converted into a home. The designer of the loft, who is also the owner, projected the internal design solutions by immediately acting upon the restructuring process. In this way, he was able to combine the theoretical aspects of the design with the practical aspects of construction. Precise compositional choices and materials characterize the project as does the simple design of the custom-made furniture, which emphasizes the ample open-space, without reducing its original size. The brick walls were repainted or covered by panels of sheetrock and an oak wood pavement was restored and used throughout the apartment, while the still-functional original tubing and the new one were left exposed. The latter also serve as supports for the industrial aluminum lamps that are accordingly arranged in the various rooms. The entrance opens on to a custom-made kitchen, which is placed next to several older pieces of furniture. As all the other permanent furnishings of the house, those in the kitchen are composed of a supporting structure of iron scaffolding beams, upon which natural wood shelves and ledges have been placed. The two libraries, which form a reading corner, mark the central part of the loft and they have been built using the same architectural solutions. In the kitchen, as in the central area and other parts of the loft, the ceiling has been interrupted by new skylights, essential geometric shapes that allow the natural light to descend from the ceiling, brightening the darker areas of the home. In addition, the light reflects the various colors that have been used to paint the interior surfaces, creating visual effects that vary according to the time of day. The house's various functions are integrated in the large open-space, which is characterized by the fixed furniture, while the bedroom, built laterally, and bathroom are separately located. The bathroom was designed according to the overall philosophy of the project, with the scaffolding beams used to support the lacquered iron tub and the glass panel, which houses the taps and the shower's colored tube.

All'ultimo piano di un edificio industriale nel Queens uno dei laboratori a pianta libera con doppio fronte finestrato è stato convertito in abitazione. Il progettista del loft, che si identifica in questo caso con il diretto fruitore, ha pensato alle soluzioni d'interni impegnandosi direttamente nella ristrutturazione, affiancando così all'aspetto teorico del disegno, l'aspetto pratico della costruzione. L'intervento si caratterizza per precise scelte compositive e materiche e per semplicità degli elementi d'arredo su disegno, chiamati in questo caso a scandire l'ampio spazio unitario senza tuttavia cancellarne la dimensione originaria. Le pareti in mattone sono state ridipinte o rivestite da pannelli in cartongesso, il pavimento di rovere è stato restaurato e riutilizzato per l'intera superficie, le vecchie tubazioni ancora attive sono state recuperate e lasciate in vista insieme a quelle dei nuovi impianti che sostengono anche le lampade industriali di alluminio, ripetute seguendo la disposizione delle diverse zone della casa. Sull'ingresso si apre la cucina che affianca ad alcuni vecchi arredi un mobile su disegno. Come tutti gli altri arredi fissi della casa, la cucina è composta da una struttura portante di tubi in ferro da ponteggio su cui si innestano piani e mensole di legno naturale. La stessa soluzione figurativa e materica è ripetuta per le due librerie che segnano la parte centrale del loft definendo una zona di lettura. Nella cucina, nella zona centrale, e in altre parti del loft, il soffitto è stato interrotto da nuovi lucernari pensati come essenziali volumi geometrici che scendono dal plafone portando, nelle zone meno luminose, nuove fonti di luce naturale enfatizzate dai diversi colori impiegati per colorarne le superfici interne che, secondo le ore del giorno, riflettono diverse tonalità cromatiche. Tutte le funzioni della casa sono integrate fra loro nello spazio unitario originario scandito dai soli arredi fissi. La camera da letto e il bagno sono invece separati in spazi indipendenti; la prima è stata ricavata in una camera laterale. Il bagno segue la filosofia dell'intervento complessivo con tubi da ponteggio impiegati per sostenere la vasca di ferro laccato e la lastra verticale di vetro dove sono fissati i rubinetti e il tubo cromato della doccia.

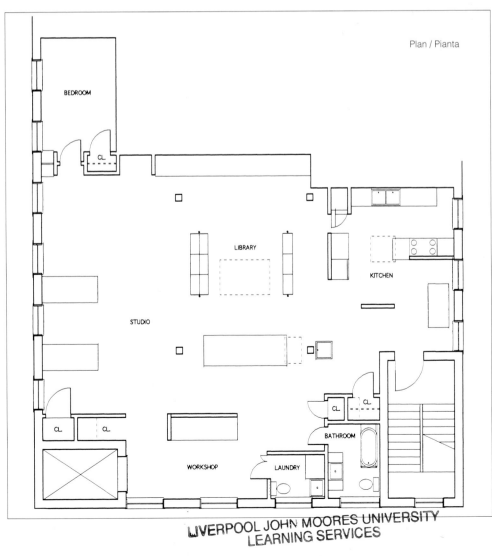

Plan / Pianta

BEDROOM

CL.

LIBRARY

KITCHEN

STUDIO

CL.

CL.

CL.

CL.

BATHROOM

WORKSHOP

LAUNDRY

ATELIER URBANO
URBAN ATELIER
Diane Lewis Architect, 1997

To create her new bi-level home-studio, Diane Lewis restructured an industrial space inside a building, built in 1880, in the Washington Square area. The old structure was characterized by large windows, which faced South, brick walls and wooden ceilings. It was viewed as a regular container and as a "historical memory", a sort of functional box to be filled with a new layout and with choices that would emphasize the living and working spaces of this home. The office was placed on the first level and furnished with large work tables, while the living area was arranged on the top level. The project's philosophy emphasized the detachment of the new elements of composition, to be used as partitions, and the building container, whose original aspect was preserved. The wooden ceiling and the brick walls were therefore painted white, neutralizing the materials and the chromatic characteristics. A brick ziggurat fireplace was added to the original exposed brick walls, completing the look of one of the living room's walls with a plasticized effect. Rather than using the standard, thin partitions, the rooms were created as architectural blocks, without doors (with the exception of the sliding panel in the bedroom). These blocks are a set of container-elements that are configured, according to their location, as small and functional rooms, but also as closets, bookshelves, ledges and lecterns, crannies and internal niches, which optimize carefully projected corners. At times, these architectural blocks are full-height, covering a part of the ceiling, though they never fully blend with it; rather, they outline their distinctiveness from it. This kind of solution was adopted for the space located above the staircase, on the first level. Here, a vertical panel separates the living room and extends upward to the ceiling, where an embedded light has been placed, to envelope the beginning of the staircase. All the architectural elements of this well-planned composition are built in gypsum, with particular attention given to the details of the fixed joint edge, that emphasizes the plastic effect. Everything has been painted white, a hue that is repeated in some of the furnishings and in the sliding curtain that shields the strong, sunny afternoon light when it penetrates the large windows, brightening the immense room.

Uno spazio industriale all'interno di un edificio del 1880 nella zona di Washington Square è stato trasformato da Diane Lewis per ospitare la sua nuova abitazione-studio su due livelli. La vecchia costruzione, caratterizzata da ampie vetrate rivolte a sud, muri in mattone e soffitti di legno è stata assunta come contenitore regolare e come 'memoria storica'; scatola edilizia in cui intervenire con la nuova disposizione funzionale e con le scelte compositive chiamate a scandire gli spazi di una casa dove vivere e lavorare. L'ufficio, con grandi tavoli di lavoro, è stato organizzato al primo livello, l'abitazione in quello sovrastante. La filosofia progettuale dell'intervento ha sottolineato il distacco tra i nuovi elementi compositivi di divisione spaziale e il contenitore edilizio, rimasto nel suo aspetto originario. Il soffitto ligneo e le pareti in mattone sono così stati verniciati di bianco, rendendone neutre le caratteristiche materiche e cromatiche. Alle preesistenti pareti di mattone faccia a vista si è aggiunto un caminetto a ziggurat dello stesso materiale, che conclude in modo plastico una parete del soggiorno. Invece dei comuni sottili tavolati divisori, le stanze sono state pensate come blocchi architettonici senza porte (ad esclusione della parete scorrevole della camera da letto), serie di elementi-contenitore che si configurano, secondo la loro ubicazione, come piccole e funzionali stanze, ma anche come armadi e librerie, mensole e leggii, nicchie e loculi interni, che valorizzano studiate visuali. A volte i blocchi architettonici si spingono sino a coprire parte del soffitto, da cui però sottolineano sempre il loro distacco. È il caso della soluzione adottata sopra il vano scala al primo piano, dove una superficie divisoria verticale, che separa dal soggiorno, prosegue sul soffitto per ospitare una luce ad incasso, avvolgendo l'arrivo della scala. Tutti gli elementi architettonici di questa studiata composizione domestica sono costruiti in cartongesso, con particolare cura nel dettaglio dello spigolo d'incastro realizzato in negativo, per valorizzarne l'effetto plastico. Tutto è tinteggiato di bianco, tonalità ripresa anche da alcuni arredi e dalla tenda scorrevole che scherma dalla luce dei pomeriggi più assolati l'ampia vetrata del luminoso soggiorno.

64

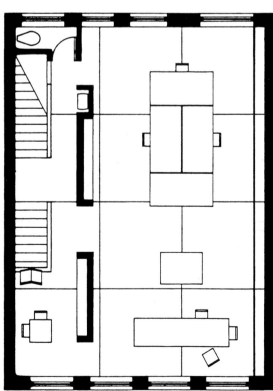

Plan for the first level / Pianta del primo livello

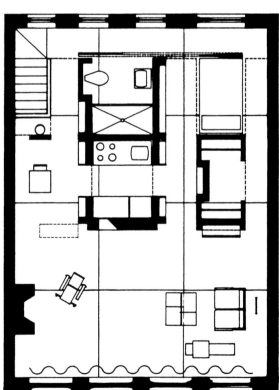

Plan for the second level / Pianta del secondo livello

READY-MADE ABITABILE
LIVEABLE READY-MADE
LOT/EK, Ada Tolla and Giuseppe Lignano Architects, 1997

In restructuring this loft, its laboratory aspect and its large unified space were maintained through the knowledgeable selection of materials and furniture. The latter are also the result of a creative transposition of composition. The cement floor, the beams and various tubing systems have been maintained and kept exposed. The many windows have been restored and painted white, like all the rest of the architectural coverings. The single partition that separates the work area from the bedroom is an important and fixed element of composition. It inclines slightly away from the windowed façade, proceeding on to the bathroom at the far end and doubling as a shelter for the shower. The latter is covered with panels of glass that allow the old walls and water pipes to be seen. This unusual wall is covered in aluminium, a ready-made solution achieved by transforming an old transportation container into a formidable domestic scene composed of panel-doors that rotate on a central pin. When the panels are closed, the bright workroom is completely separated from the bedroom, allowing the technological equipment to emerge from the metal surface, much like in sculpture, as though each piece were an objet trouvé. When the panels are rotated, however, the areas of the loft are integrated, creating a more domestic aspect. Next to the sink there is a small storage area and above the stove, the shelves exemplify a well-designed kitchen. The far wall of the bedroom is covered by a row of metal closets and office cabinets of various colours and sizes, arranged in a manner that resembles a patchwork. This same brilliant philosophy of composition characterises the "equipped island" that is the central work area. The entire architectural scheme is supported by a well-planned composition of old, white refrigerators placed horizontally and transformed into furniture-containers. One of the largest doors has been turned into an additional work area by adding support shelves to it. This lab-home has been designed as a refined prefab composed of industrial objects, whose functions have been somewhat distorted.

Il carattere di laboratorio e la dimensione di spazio unitario di questo loft sono stati mantenuti nella scelta dei materiali e degli arredi, questi ultimi frutto di una sapiente e creativa trasposizione compositiva. Il pavimento in cemento è stato conservato insieme alle travi e agli impianti a vista del soffitto; le ampie finestre sono state recuperate e tinteggiate di bianco come tutto l'involucro architettonico. Un unico forte elemento compositivo separa la zona di lavoro dalla camera da letto, ponendosi come quinta fissa di riferimento, leggermente inclinata rispetto alla facciata finestrata per proseguire e concludersi nel locale bagno sul fondo, fungendo da riparo per la doccia rivestita con lastre di vetro che lasciano a vista i vecchi muri e i tubi dell'acqua. Questa inusitata parete attrezzata di alluminio si propone come riuscito ready-made che ha trasformato un lato di un container da trasporto in una formidabile scena domestica composta da pannelli-porte che ruotano su un perno centrale. Se i pannelli sono chiusi la luminosa sala di lavoro è separata completamente dalla zona notte, lasciando però emergere, come in una composizione scultorea, le attrezzature tecnologiche che escono dalla superficie metallica come degli objets trouvé. Una volta ruotati i pannelli, le zone del loft si integrano denunciando l'aspetto più domestico dell'abitazione: di fianco al lavello è organizzato un piccolo magazzino, mentre sopra il fornello sono disposte le mensole di una piccola e attrezzata cucina. La parete di fondo della camera da letto è occupata da armadi metallici e cassettiere per ufficio di diverso colore e dimensione, sovrapposte a formare un efficace patchwork di arredi. Questa stessa brillante filosofia compositiva caratterizza anche 'l'isola attrezzata' di lavoro centrale. I piani di lavoro sono sostenuti da uno studiato incastro di vecchi frigoriferi bianchi posti in orizzontale e trasformati in mobile-contenitore. Uno degli sportelli più grandi diventa un ulteriore piano di lavoro, grazie all'applicazione di due nuove mensole di sostegno. Una casa-laboratorio pensata come un raffinato ready-made di oggetti industriali, più o meno stravolti dalla loro funzione.

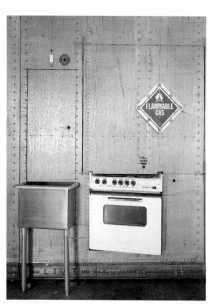

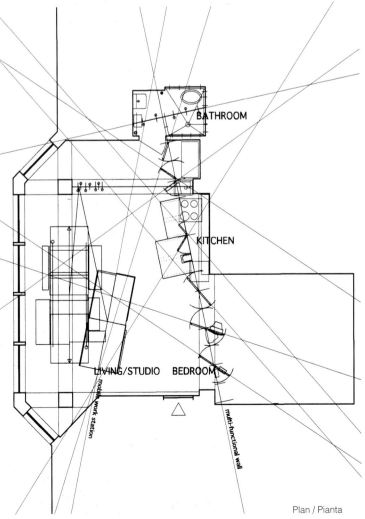

Plan / Pianta

TARE
MAX.C.W
MAX.G.W
CU.CAP

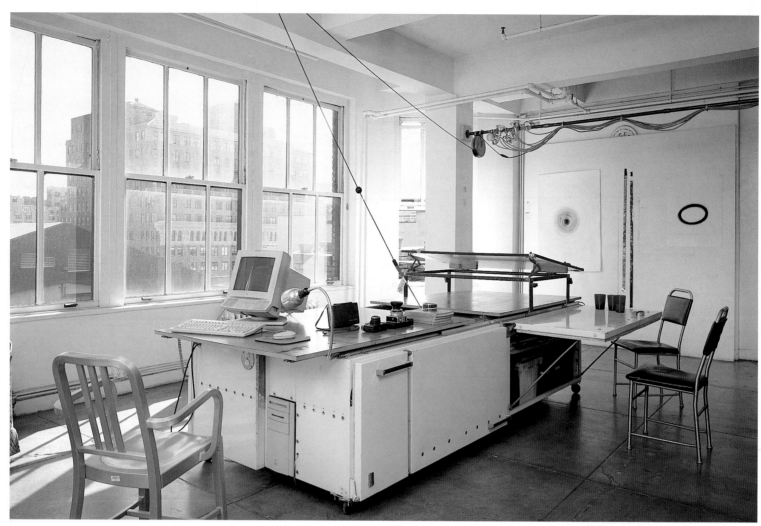

ORIENTAL FLAVORS
Smith and Thompson Architects, 1995

This unusual two-level loft, built on the last floor of an industrial build-ing, was created for a professional couple who had previously lived in Japan. The interior restructuring was inspired by the refined sim-plicity of the figures and the rare atmosphere of the domestic spaces that are typical of the Land of the Rising Sun. The floor space of the room on the top level corresponds to that of the roof, which has been converted into a terrace-garden. This loft is characterized by the luminosity of its open-space and the ample windows in its walls, the largest of which offers an exceptional view of the Chrysler and Empire State Buildings, symbols of the city. The restructuring project, therefore, arranged the various living spaces in a manner that would emphasize this view, organizing the passages in ways that would optimize the panorama afforded by the central living area. This cen-tral room is separated from the entrance by a sliding pane located next to the maple wood stairway. Its length and narrowness are rem-iniscent of the original loft, as is the original brick wall in the kitchen, which remains exposed in certain sections. The kitchen opens onto the dining room, at the end of which there is a central fireplace made of coarse sheeting and built according to a ziggurat motif. It rests against a wall covered with regular slabs of maple wood, which effi-ciently complete the scenic element of the composition. The night area, placed in front of the stairway, is shielded by a small vestibule that guarantees full privacy. The reference to a Japanese style of interior decor is provided not only by the use of natural wood, set in basic geometrical patterns and used as shelves and surfaces, but also by the careful attention in creating storage spaces and containers. The ones located under the steps of the stairway are of particular interest. These functional drawers are of various sizes and depths, eliminating the need for handles. In addition, they serve as an abstract decorative element. The wooden stools in the bathroom also function as storage space, as do the small parallelepiped containers that rest on the oak floor, hiding the stereo system's wiring.

All'ultimo piano di una costruzione industriale è stato ricavato questo inconsueto loft su due livelli per una coppia di professionisti che avevano precedentemente vissuto in Giappone. Al Paese del Sol Levante, alla raffinata semplicità delle sue figure e alle rarefatte atmosfere dei suoi spazi domestici si sono ispirati i progettisti nel definire i riferimenti compositivi di questo proget-to d'interni. Il loft, con una stanza al piano superiore corrispondente alla quota del tetto piano trasformato in terrazza-giardino, si presentava come un luminoso spazio unitario con tutti e tre i muri perimetrali segnati da ampie aperture. Il lato maggiore offriva un'eccezionale vista sul Chrysler e sull'Empire State Buildings, i due grattacieli simbolo della città. La soluzione proget-tuale ha quindi distribuito i diversi spazi enfatizzando questa visuale, organizzando i percorsi in modo da offrire al meglio il panorama urbano verso cui si rivolge la grande zona giorno. Questa, separata dall'ingresso tramite una vetrata scorrevole affiancata alla scala di legno d'acero, ricor-da, nella sua dimensione stretta e lunga, il carattere del loft originario, anche grazie ad alcuni brani parietali in mattone, lasciati a vista nella cucina aperta verso la zona pranzo. Sul fondo, un camino centrale in lamiera grezza, costruito secondo un motivo a ziqqurat, poggia sulla parete rivestita con lastre regolari di legno d'acero, come efficace elemento scenografico conclusivo. La zona notte è stata ricavata di fronte alla scala, schermata da un piccolo vestibolo che ne garantisce l'assoluta privacy. Oltre al legno naturale, impiegato secondo geometrie elementari e incastri di piani e superfici ben governati, ciò che ricorda la dimensione domestica giapponese è l'attenzione rivolta alla creazione di ripostigli e contenitori. Di particolare interesse quelli rica-vati sotto i gradini della scala, funzionali cassetti di diversa dimensione che, grazie alla loro dif-ferente profondità, evitano l'uso delle maniglie, configurandosi anche come elementi decorativi astratti. Contenitori di legno sono anche gli sgabelli del bagno e i piccoli parallelepipedi che nel soggiorno nascondono l'impianto stereo, fluttuando sul pavimento a listoni di rovere. che li sostiene.

74

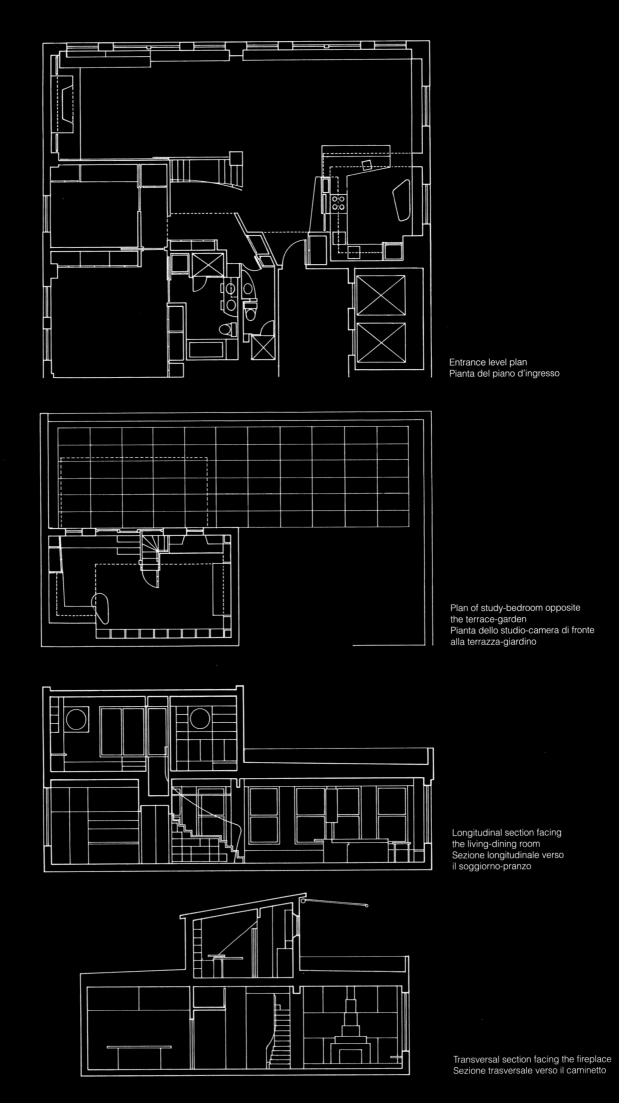

Entrance level plan
Pianta del piano d'ingresso

Plan of study-bedroom opposite
the terrace-garden
Pianta dello studio-camera di fronte
alla terrazza-giardino

Longitudinal section facing
the living-dining room
Sezione longitudinale verso
il soggiorno-pranzo

Transversal section facing the fireplace
Sezione trasversale verso il caminetto

IL VALORE DELLO SPAZIO
THE VALUE OF SPACE
Studio MORSA, 1991

This loft, which overlooks New York City's skyline, is located inside an industrial high-rise on Broadway. It has been converted into a luxurious apartment by conserving its unified space and optimizing the brightness provided by large, regular, vertical windows. The vast, open-space area was considered to be valuable in itself and was, therefore, used as a primary object of composition in the new layout, without, however, sacrificing the essential privacy of the sleeping quarters, to which a study was adjoined. The bathrooms and closets were placed along the only blind wall, where the elevator and stairway are also located. The natural oak panels used to cover the closets is a brilliant disguise, extending out to uniformly cover the entrance and bathroom doors. These panels express a universality of space, their image efficiently providing a split from the loft's previous industrial purpose. The pine green slabs that characterize the master bathroom, along with those in Serene stone used in the flooring of the main room, define the exclusive and carefully studied character of the new accommodation, a style that is further emphasized by the original Doric columns. The kitchen, created with a double counter in natural wood, opens onto the dining room. Coupled with the geometrically imposing wall at the back of the room, the kitchen is a completing element. The wall separates the day area from the study and from the furnished hallway, which leads to the master bedroom at the end. The latter is completely covered by a modern paneling in natural oak. The wall at the end of the kitchen flanks a sandblasted glass panel next to a sliding panel of white fabric, which is arranged in a pattern of rectangular shapes, placed between two glass panes. It is a sort of "fixed tent", reminiscent of the interior decorating style of traditional Japanese houses. The carefully selected objects and furnishings also provide an Oriental and Mediterranean ambience. Foremost among them is the red piece of furniture, which emanates a taste of the Orient, and the Spanish jars that have been strategically placed throughout.

Un loft affacciato sul panorama newyorkese dai piani alti di un edificio industriale di Broadway è stato convertito in un lussuoso appartamento conservandone al meglio lo spazio unitario, illuminato da una serie regolare di ampie finestre verticali. Il valore dello spazio, assunto come qualità a sé stante, è sottolineato con convinzione e abile regia compositiva nella nuova sistemazione planimetrica che ha saputo però garantire la necessaria privacy della zona notte affiancata da un piccolo studio. Lungo l'unica parete cieca, dove si trova il blocco scala e gli ascensori, sono stati organizzati i servizi e degli utili armadi-ripostiglio a tutt'altezza che nascondono la loro funzione grazie al rivestimento in pannelli di quercia naturale che inglobano in un'unica superficie

materica anche le porte di accesso e quelle dei bagni. Questi esprimono nella loro immagine il carattere dell'intero spazio che a livello globale produce un efficace slittamento rispetto all'antica funzione industriale. Insieme alle lastre di marmo Verde Alpi che caratterizzano il rivestimento del bagno padronale, quelle di pietra Serena, impiegate come pavimentazione della zona giorno, denunciano il carattere esclusivo e attentamente calibrato della nuova abitazione, scandita anche dalla preesistenza delle forti colonne doriche. La cucina, pensata come doppio bancone di legno naturale, aperta sulla zona pranzo, si pone come elemento conclusivo insieme alla composizione geometrica che caratterizza la parete alle sue spalle. Questa separa la zona giorno dallo studio e dal corridoio attrezzato che conduce alla camera da letto sul fondo, interamente rivestita con una moderna boiserie di quercia naturale. La quinta architettonica alle spalle della cucina affianca una lastra di vetro sabbiato a una parete scorrevole che, dal pavimento al soffitto, organizza una sequenza di rettangoli regolari in tessuto bianco posti tra due lastre di vetro, proponendosi come sorta di riuscita 'tenda fissa' che ricorda gli interni delle case giapponesi tradizionali. Sapori orientali e mediterranei provengono anche dall'accurata selezione di arredi e oggetti, da cui emergono il mobile rosso di sapore cinese e la collezione di grandi giare spagnole distribuite con cura in tutta la zona giorno.

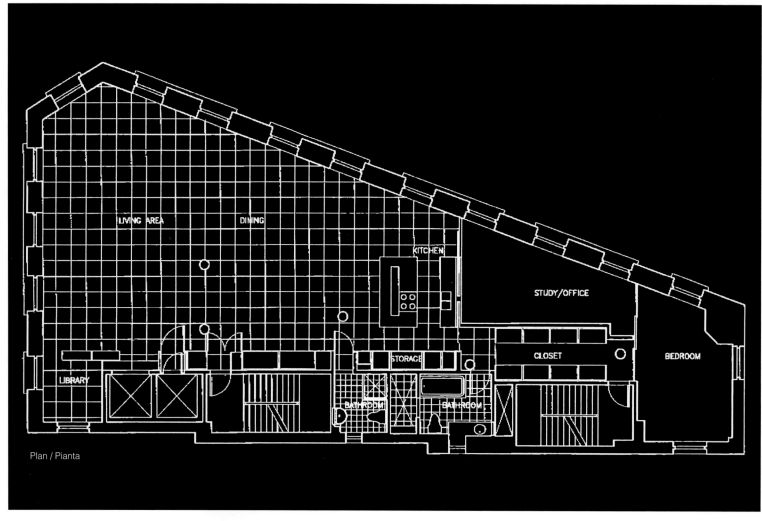

Plan / Pianta

SPACES IN LINE

In a typical industrial building of the Tribeca neighborhood, a loft has been restructured and converted into living space. The two windowed façades are a fortunate anomaly compared with other constructions of this type, allowing the new layout to be designed with less restrictions and problems. The original structures used as the focal pivot point of the restructuring were the wooden beams of the ceiling and the set of five iron columns used as support for the steel beam. The metallic beam, which marks the length of the loft, was used as a guidepost along which the new rooms were designed. From the entrance, the long corridor is characterized by the columns, which have been painted dark green. A small study and the bathrooms have been placed in an area that extends well past the loft's midpoint and is situated between the metallic structure and the blind wall. The kitchen, which opens onto the ample open-space area, is also located in this zone. Since this area lacks natural light, specific solutions were used to create the desired living standards. The small study, for example, was completely covered in wood and equipped with a sliding door, covered with the same material and comprised of overlayed large glass panels. This allows the study to be connected to the open-area when the door is opened, or to be separated from it when it is closed. A ceiling light, designed to function as an artificial skylight, provides the perfect solution to the lack of natural lighting. A cherry wood parquet covers all the floors of the loft, except in the kitchen. Here, the floor has been covered with sheets of light granite, which is also used for the shelves above the counter and around the sink. The latter is encased in a specifically designed natural wood cabinet. The night area, placed along the windowed wall, faces the study and the closet. The bedroom guarantees total privacy. It has an adjoining bathroom, which is completely covered in botticino marble and richly decorated. The solution used in this loft's design includes the covering of the ceiling with a false ceiling, used to conceal the original structure, which, however, remains exposed in the brightly lit day area located against the main façade.

In un tipico edificio industriale del quartiere di Tribeca, è stato ristrutturato e convertito in abitazione uno dei loft sovrapposti. La presenza di due pareti finestrate, una fortunata anomalia rispetto ad altre costruzioni di questo tipo, ha permesso di studiare la nuova distribuzione in modo meno vincolante e problematico. Le preesistenze cui fare riferimento nel progetto erano i travetti in legno del soffitto e la serie di cinque colonne in ferro, di sostegno alla trave dello stesso materiale. La significativa struttura metallica, che percorre in modo longitudinale tutta la lunghezza del loft, è stata assunta come elemento architettonico lungo cui organizzare, in linea, le nuove stanze dell'abitazione. Dall'ingresso si coglie il lungo corridoio scandito dalle colonne tinteggiate verde scuro. Nella zona compresa tra la struttura metallica e la parete cieca, per una lunghezza che si estende oltre la metà del loft, sono stati organizzati, in linea, degli spazi di servizio, uno studiolo e la cucina aperta sull'ampia zona giorno. Questa fascia priva di luce naturale è stata sfruttata al meglio con soluzioni che hanno creato ricercate qualità abitative. Il piccolo studio, ad esempio, è stato completamente rivestito di legno e la parete scorrevole, dello stesso materiale con ampie lastre di vetro acidato, permette, quando aperta, di collegare il confortevole studiolo allo spazio complessivo. Una luce a soffitto, pensata come sorta di artificiale lucernario, risponde in modo brillante all'oggettiva assenza di aperture. Il parquet in legno di ciliegio copre l'intera superficie del loft ad eccezione della cucina, segnata dalle lastre di granito chiaro, materiale ripetuto per i piani di appoggio del bancone e per l'alzata del lavello nel mobile di legno naturale su disegno. La zona notte è organizzata di fronte allo studio e alla cabina armadio, lungo la parete finestrata. La camera da letto, affiancata da un bagno indipendente rivestito in Botticino e riccamente decorato, garantisce l'assoluta privacy. La nuova soluzione progettuale si esprime anche nel controsoffitto impiegato in tutta la zona suddivisa in stanze, per nascondere la struttura originaria del soffitto che invece torna in luce nella luminosa zona giorno, organizzata sul fronte principale.

Plan / Pianta
1. Living Room / Soggiorno   5. Master Bathroom / Bagno Padronale
2. Dining Room / Sala da Pranzo 6. Bedroom / Camera da letto
3. Kitchen / Cucina   7. Laundry Room / Lavanderia
4. Study / Studio   8. Guest Bathroom / Bagno

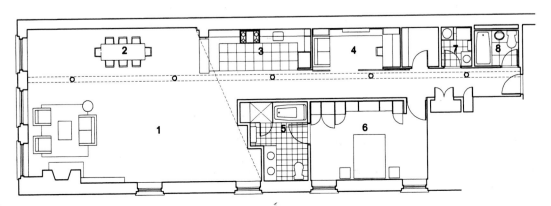

92

One of the superimposed lofts in an industrial building in the Tribeca neighborhood has been restructured and converted into a big apartment. Characterized by its large, unified and regularly-shaped open-space area, the day zone is located against the central façade, which is marked by four windows, placed side by side. The loft's original size is maintained, but its industrial and commercial warehouse aspect have been transformed through the choice of building materials and furnishings. The entrance, flanked by a guest bathroom and the laundry room, located against the blind wall, opens onto the open-space. Like the bathrooms and the kitchen, it is characterized by a pavement made of light stones, which is then interrupted by a parquet of cherry wood girders placed horizontally along the wider spaces, emphasizing the longitudinal perspective. This emphasis is also provided by the original, cylindrical iron columns that support the beams, which run along the entire length of the day area. Here, the ceiling beams have also been left exposed and have been painted white. Past the useful storage area that flanks the entrance, the blind wall at the left is optimized as a useful bookshelf that extends to the end of the wall, uninterrupted by the full-height, black marble fireplace. The fireplace serves as a reference point of composition, influencing the style of furniture used in the living room. The dining room, located within the open-space area, faces the kitchen, which, in turn, appears to be a separate entity but is, in reality, a part of the whole, unified space. The large counter with granite shelves contoured in steel and flanked by four breakfast stools is a distinct emphatic element, separating the dining room from the kitchen with the aid of the sloping ceiling that leads to the night area at the far end. The large bedroom guarantees complete privacy. It is adjoined to an attentively designed bathroom and it is furnished with a large closet. The entire night area, with its windowed wall, is a precious addition to the comprehensive livable open space-area in which living room, dining room, library and kitchen are a successful harmony of multifunctional spaces.

94

Uno dei loft sovrapposti di un edificio industriale nel quartiere di Tribeca è stato ristrutturato e convertito in un ampio appartamento caratterizzato dal grande spazio aperto, unitario e regolare, della zona giorno. Questa, rivolta sul fronte principale segnato da quattro finestre affiancate, mantiene la dimensione originaria del loft, stravolgendo tuttavia l'aspetto di magazzino e ogni antica vocazione industriale, grazie alle soluzioni materiche e compositive adottate. L'ingresso, affiancato da un bagno di servizio e dalla lavanderia disposti lungo il muro cieco, è direttamente affacciato sullo spazio unitario. La pavimentazione di pietra chiara segna l'ingresso, la zona servizi e la cucina, per poi interrompersi in prossimità del parquet di ciliegio a doghe, posato in parallelo ai lati maggiori del loft, enfatizzandone così la prospettiva longitudinale. Questa è valorizzata anche dalla struttura di ferro preesistente, composta da quattro colonne cilindriche a sostegno della trave che corre per tutta la lunghezza della zona giorno, dove è stata lasciata a vista anche la serie di travi in legno del soffitto, tinteggiate di bianco. Dopo un utile ripostiglio che affianca l'ingresso, la parete cieca di sinistra è sfruttata come essenziale libreria continua, interrotta dal camino a tutt'altezza rivestito di marmo nero; episodio compositivo di riferimento che organizza la disposizione degli arredi del salotto. La zona pranzo, ricavata all'interno dello spazio aperto complessivo, è disposta di fronte alla cucina su disegno proposta come luogo compiuto e definito, ma parte di quello unitario generale. Un bancone, dai piani di granito e con profili di acciaio di sostegno, è affiancato da quattro sgabelli per il breakfast, ponendosi come elemento di scansione tra zona pranzo e cucina, insieme al ribassamento del soffitto che prosegue verso la zona notte ricavata sul fondo. L'ampia camera da letto, corredata da un bagno indipendente attentamente disegnato e da una generosa cabina armadio, garantisce l'assoluta privacy. L'intera zona notte, con parete finestrata, si configura come prezioso ampliamento abitabile dello spazio aperto complessivo, dove soggiorno, pranzo, biblioteca e cucina, sono affiancati in una riuscita sintesi multifunzionale.

Plan / Pianta
1. Living Room
   Soggiorno
2. Dining Room
   Sala da Pranzo
3. Kitchen / Cucina
4. Laundry Room
   Lavanderia
5. Bathroom / Bagno
6. Master Bathroom
   Bagno Padronale
7. Bedroom
   Camera da letto
8. Closet / Ripostiglio

95

LOFTS

APARTMENTS

SPAZI ASSOLUTI
ABSOLUTE SPACES
Gabellini Associates, 1998

A large apartment overlooking Park Avenue and surrounded by large terraces is the home of a collector of black and white photographs. The colors and materials used to create this refined living space were influenced by the monochromatic tones of the photographs, which have been exposed with great care throughout the apartment. Square panels of light stone, a meter in depth, characterize the sequence of the rooms with great rigor. The rooms are separated from each other by several original partitions and by new, large panels in mahogany that double in their function, acting as items of decor and storage containers. The bright living room is the principal area of the house. It is connected to the foyer-exposition gallery, which leads to the night area on one side and to the study and dining room on the other. The bedroom overlooks a terrace, which functions as a plein air extension of the room. A full-height mahogany panel, interrupted only by a photograph at its center, functions as the bed's monolithic head rest, hiding the closet located behind it. The master bathroom is a kind of magical and ethereal living box, completely covered in slabs of white Sivec marble. It is characterized by two glass panels, which can be rendered opaque electronically, allowing the area to be either visible or invisible from the bedroom. A single slab of white marble is also used to define the linear sink, supported by an essential steel structure. An additional vertical panel, also in mahogany, emerges from the whiteness of the walls and ceilings, to separate the dining room from the study. Here, too, the wooden container-panel functions as a frame for a photograph of the collection. It is interrupted by a thick, metal supporting ledge, an element that is repeated on the square, stone table centrally positioned in the dining room. The absolutely clean cut of the design, the rigorous choice of materials and furnishings and the careful attention given to the display of the photographs makes this project a truly successful merge between domestic reality and an art gallery. The apartment provides a sequence of 'absolute spaces' that are carefully planned, from a functional viewpoint, and strongly characterized by their architectural design.

100

Un grande appartamento affacciato su Park Avenue e circondato da ampie terrazze ospita l'abitazione di un collezionista di fotografie in bianco e nero. Le tonalità monocrome delle stampe, collocate con attenta regia espositiva in ogni spazio della casa, hanno suggerito la palette di riferimento e le tonalità relative all'impiego dei materiali per definire l'immagine complessiva di questo raffinato spazio domestico. Lastre quadrate di pietra chiara di un metro di lato scandiscono con estremo rigore la sequenza delle stanze, separate tra loro da alcuni tavolati esistenti e da nuovi forti setti in mogano, impiegati anche come arredi contenitori. Il luminoso soggiorno

Axonometric View
Esploso prospettico

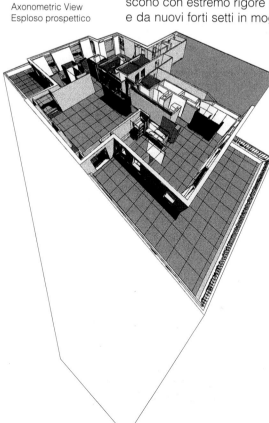

si pone come spazio centrale della casa, anticipato da un foyer-galleria espositiva che porta da un lato alla zona notte, dall'altro allo studio e alla zona pranzo. Nella camera da letto, affacciata su un terrazzo che ne costituisce un diretto prolungamento en plein air, una parete in mogano a tutt'altezza, interrotta da una fotografia centrale, si pone come monolitica testata del letto nascondendo alle sue spalle la cabina armadio. Il bagno padronale, pensato come magica ed eterea scatola abitabile, è caratterizzato da due pareti vetrate opacizzate in modo elettronico, che permettono, rispetto alla camera da letto, di nascondere o rivelare a piacimento lo spazio interno, interamente rivestito con lastre di marmo bianco Sivec. Materiale impiegato in lastra unica anche per definire il lineare lavabo sostenuto da un'essenziale struttura di acciaio. Nella zona un ulteriore elemento verticale rivestito in mogano separa la sala da pranzo dallo studio emergendo dal bianco che copre pareti e soffitti. Il setto-contenitore ligneo incornicia anche in questo caso una fotografia della collezione ed è interrotto da una mensola metallica di sostegno a forte spessore che si rapporta al tavolo da pranzo quadrato centrale in pietra. L'assoluta pulizia compositiva dell'insieme, la rigorosa selezione di arredi e materiali, l'attenzione rivolta all'esposizione delle fotografie, fanno di questo progetto d'interni una riuscita commistione tra dimensione domestica e galleria d'arte. Una successione di 'spazi assoluti', attentamente calibrati dal punto di vista funzionale e fortemente caratterizzati nella loro cifra architettonica.

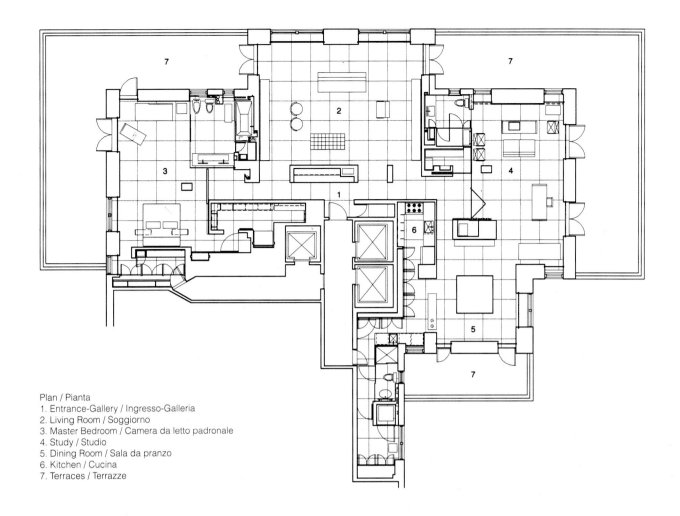

Plan / Pianta
1. Entrance-Gallery / Ingresso-Galleria
2. Living Room / Soggiorno
3. Master Bedroom / Camera da letto padronale
4. Study / Studio
5. Dining Room / Sala da pranzo
6. Kitchen / Cucina
7. Terraces / Terrazze

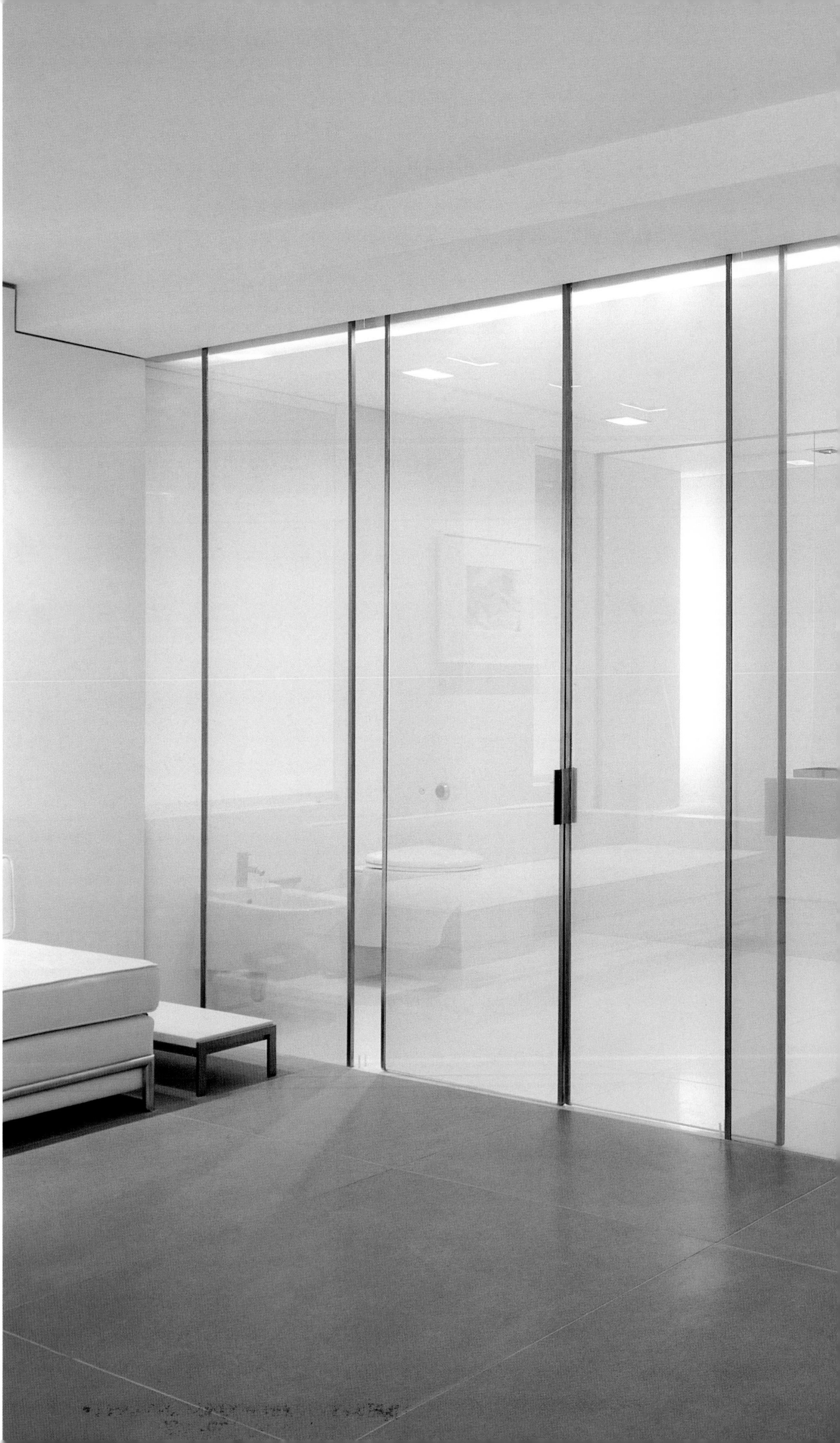

103

MANIPOLAZIONI ASIMMETRICHE
ASYMMETRIC MANIPULATIONS
Gwathmey Siegel & Associates Architects, 1997

This traditional apartment has been radically altered by optimizing the full surface area, thereby giving it a new domestic function. The open-space layout dominated and guided the project's design, rendering it similar to a loft, albeit of an exclusive type, due to the careful selection of materials and furnishing. The project's overall structure is noticeable from the start, on the external landing. Here, the blind wall has been covered with regular stone slabs set in a frame, which is illuminated by an indirect light. The slab closest to the entrance has been replaced by a mirror, which enlivens the image. As is typical of lofts, the apartment is characterized by three large, cylindrical columns and exposed ceiling rafters. Once the original partitions were eliminated, the space provided new architectural opportunities for delineating the new projected spaces. A skilled asymmetric manipulation rotated the movement of passages, creating a new perspective of the entire layout. The principal change was the diagonal positioning of the pavement's light-colored stone slabs, creating novel reference points for the new layout. To the right of the entrance, a partition separates a small studio from the large asymmetric space, the starting point of the composition. The guest bathroom conceals the custom-made kitchen, which opens onto the ample dining room and the adjoining living room. To the left, a curved, double wall in maple separates the living room from the library, drawing attention to the back of the room, where an undulating plastic wall dominates the architectural perspective. This latter plastic partition embellishes the centrally located fireplace, which is indirectly lit by a continuous border in the lower ceiling. Maple wood is also used in some of the other decorative panels, such as those that complete the large closets in the night area and the immense alcove-headboard in the bedroom. In order to preserve the feeling of the open-space, the wooden panels, which are used throughout the apartment, never fully touch the ceiling; rather, they are equipped with glass extensions, which guarantee privacy without, however, reducing the amount of available space.

108

La radicale trasformazione di un tradizionale appartamento ha definito un nuovo paesaggio domestico che, nella valorizzazione dell'intera superficie come spazio unitario, ha caratterizzato la soluzione progettuale avvicinandola a quella di un loft, seppure di tipo esclusivo, per scelta materica e per le ricercate figure d'interni. L'intervento denuncia un completo controllo progettuale già dal pianerottolo esterno, la cui parete cieca è stata rivestita con lastre di pietra regolari concluse da un essenziale cornicione, che ospita un'efficace fascia di luce indiretta. Uno specchio sostituisce una delle lastre in prossimità dell'ingresso all'abitazione vivacizzando il rivestimento. Come in un loft, l'interno denuncia la propria struttura con tre forti colonne cilindriche e con le travi a vista del soffitto. Liberato lo spazio dalle suddivisioni preesistenti, la scatola architettonica strutturale è stata assunta come spazio dove costruire una nuova architettura composta da elementi indipendenti. Una sapiente e governata manipolazione asimmetrica ha ruotato l'andamento dei percorsi e delle nuove prospettive; anzitutto posando in diagonale le lastre di pietra chiara del pavimento che indicano nuove linee di riferimento per la disposizione planimetrica. Sulla destra dell'ingresso, dopo un setto che separa da un piccolo studio, si sviluppa il volume asimmetrico centrale, dove è stato ubicato un bagno di servizio, che nasconde la cucina su disegno aperta sull'ampia zona pranzo connessa al soggiorno. Sulla sinistra una doppia parete attrezzata in curva su disegno si pone come elemento architettonico ligneo per dividere il soggiorno dalla biblioteca, segnando fortemente la prospettiva verso la parete ondulata sul fondo; un elemento plastico scandito dall'essenziale caminetto centrale e illuminato in modo indiretto da una fascia continua ottenuta nel ribassamento del soffitto. Il legno d'acero, impiegato per la facciata domestica in curva, è ripetuto per altri elementi divisori: come le ampie cabine armadio della zona notte e la grande testata-alcova della camera da letto. Per conservare la sensazione di spazio unitario i volumi lignei non raggiungono mai il soffitto e sono conclusi da lastre di vetro che, garantendo la necessaria privacy, non interrompono lo spazio. metrico e plastico.

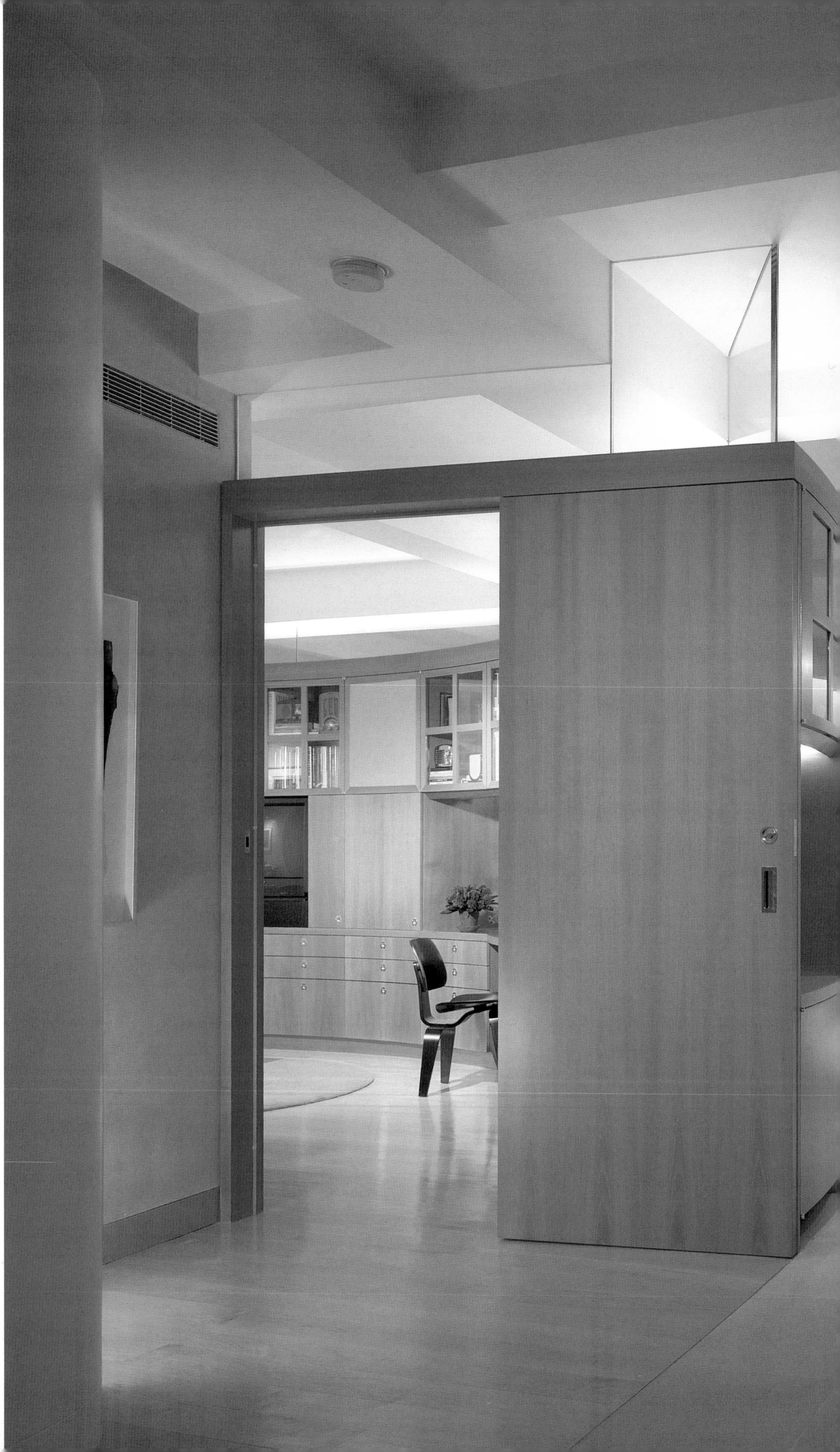

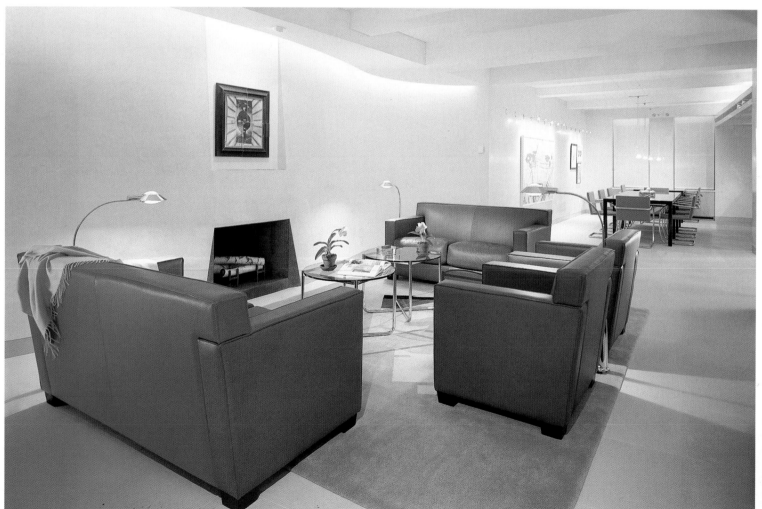

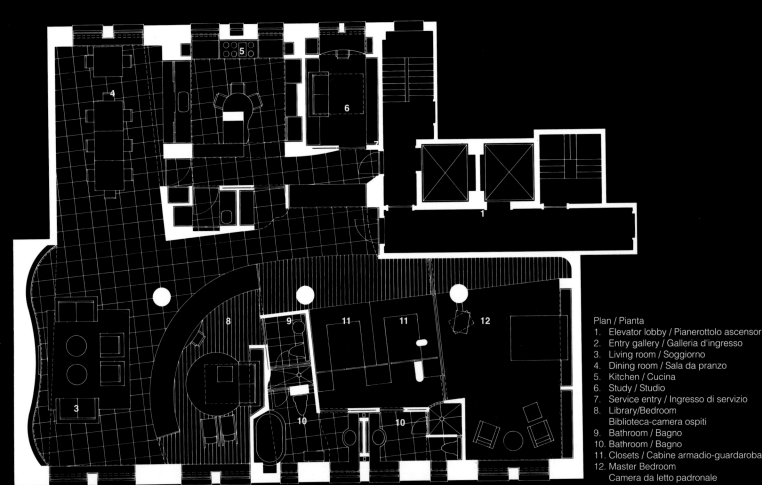

Plan / Pianta
1. Elevator lobby / Pianerottolo ascensori
2. Entry gallery / Galleria d'ingresso
3. Living room / Soggiorno
4. Dining room / Sala da pranzo
5. Kitchen / Cucina
6. Study / Studio
7. Service entry / Ingresso di servizio
8. Library/Bedroom
   Biblioteca-camera ospiti
9. Bathroom / Bagno
10. Bathroom / Bagno
11. Closets / Cabine armadio-guardaroba
12. Master Bedroom
    Camera da letto padronale

LUCE E COLORE
LIGHT AND COLOR
Ken Kennedy Architect, 1998

An apartment in Midtown was renovated to create a new living space for an Australian-born professional who works in the publishing field. The owner expressed the need for a home that would be bright and functional, as well as suitable for receiving guests and clients. The original layout divided the available space into several separate rooms, creating dark spaces without taking advantage of the natural light from the south façade. The project, therefore, eliminated all the internal panels of the apartment, transforming it into an open-space, characterized by various compositional episodes, as well as by different functional solutions. To the left of the entrance, a series of sliding panels in walnut isolate the bedroom, extending out to cover the only bathroom's wall. Same-sized panels in maple wood conceal the large closet located at the front of the bedroom, covering the full surface of this room, as well as an entire wall in the dining room, creating a very characteristic look. This solution provides the decor for an elegant entrance hall during the day, which discreetly separates the night area. A bright light crowns the wooden panels, exalting their texture. The partition that originally separated the living room from the dining room was removed, creating a new, large and luminous open-space day zone. The dark brown and brick red hues used on parts of the ceiling match the hues in the Australian artwork displayed throughout the apartment, providing a very scenic effect. The collection of furniture in the day zone and in the hallway are pieces from the Modern Movement, while the marble used for the fireplace was maintained to create an efficient and formal stylistic contrast. A series of bright and colorful rays, created by projecting colored lights onto the white ceiling, cut through the kitchen furniture, allowing a number of different atmospheres to permeate and determine the environment's ambience. The colors of the lights can be altered, according to the desired effect and the time of day. This is a very efficient solution and one that expresses a refined creativity, paralleling the colored illumination of the Empire State Building, one of the city's symbols par excellence, which changes its colors monthly.

Un appartamento della Midtown è stato rinnovato per ospitare l'abitazione di una professionista impegnata nel mercato editoriale. Le esigenze espresse dalla committenza erano quelle di possedere una casa luminosa e funzionale, in grado anche di presentarsi come interno per ricevere clienti e ospiti. La distribuzione planimetrica esistente divideva lo spazio disponibile in diverse piccole stanze, creando zone buie, senza sfruttare al meglio la luce della facciata sud. L'intervento ha così liberato dai tavolati interni tutta la casa, trasformandola in uno spazio unitario, scandito però da compiuti episodi compositivi e da diverse soluzioni funzionali. Sulla sinistra una serie di pannelli scorrevoli in noce separa la camera da letto dall'ingresso, per coprire poi la parete dell'unico bagno centrale. Pannelli della stessa dimensione, ma in legno d'acero, nascondono di fronte alla camera da letto l'ampia cabina armadio per rivestire tutto il perimetro sino a caratterizzare un lato della sala da pranzo. Questa soluzione permette durante il giorno di creare un elegante corridoio d'ingresso che separa la zona notte in modo discreto. Una fascia luminosa di coronamento sottolinea il senso di superficie compiuta data al rivestimento ligneo. L'ampia zona giorno, liberata dal tavolato di divisione, unisce in un luminoso ambiente unitario sala da pranzo e soggiorno. Di grande effetto il colore impiegato in alcune zone del soffitto, marrone scuro e rosso mattone, che vogliono riprendere le tonalità delle opere d'arte australiane (paese d'origine della proprietaria) che sono distribuite in tutta la casa. Una collezione di mobili del Movimento Moderno arreda la zona giorno e il corridoio, mentre il vecchio camino di marmo è stato conservato per costituire un efficace contrappunto stilistico e formale. Una serie di sorgenti luminose colorate interrompe il mobile della cucina permettendo di configurare diverse atmosfere grazie ai colori delle luci proiettate sul soffitto bianco: luci colorate che possono essere selezionate secondo le esigenze e le ore del giorno. Una soluzione di grande efficacia che esprime una raffinata creatività anche nel riferimento all'illuminazione colorata dell'Empire State Building, che ogni mese cambia l'aspetto notturno di uno dei simboli urbani per eccellenza.

124

Plan / Pianta

SUPERFICI ARCHITETTONICHE
ARCHITECTURAL SURFACES
Gerner Kronick + Valcarcel, Architects PC, 1997

This traditional apartment, overlooking Central Park, was the subject of radical restructuring project that transformed the original decor and structure with a certain creative sensibility. The result was the creation of an image of superb comfort and modernity. The large open-space day area was obtained by removing the original partitions, leaving only the pillars and ceiling beams exposed, setting up the new layout longitudinally. This area is distinguished by various compositional elements that emphasize the view of the park. The entrance opens onto the dining room, which is virtually delineated by a pillar and by the exposed rafters of the ceiling. On the left, the bright living room, which overlooks Central Park, is flanked by the study, which is hidden by a sliding partition and another panel, used as a storage closet. The open-space area, which houses the living room and dining room, is further characterized by a large, curved piece of furniture covered in square slabs of travertine, a figurative element that also serves as a closet for the night area, which is located directly behind it. The regular, geometric shapes of the stone covering act as a reference point for the material used in many of the other rooms, such as in the wood paneling of the study. As well, it is used as a cozy surface behind the bed in the master bedroom and as a decorative motif on the container-furniture, which characterizes the entire façade that extends from the front of the dining room to the kitchen. A bedroom with an independent bathroom flanks the latter. This refined succession of architectural surfaces defines the apartment's image, outlining the internal passages and perspectives and carefully balancing the available space. The result is a well-designed separation of the apartment's private spaces (the study and bedroom). Much attention was also given to the selection of materials (light wood for the pavement and precious marble mosaics for the bathroom) and furniture, some of which was custom-made. The bedroom furniture and the desk in the study, with its steel legs and wood table, are examples. Every detail is carefully planned, creating a well-orchestrated overall arrangement.

Un tradizionale appartamento affacciato su Central Park, è stato oggetto di una radicale trasformazione progettuale. L'intervento ha saputo reinventare con sensibilità creativa il decoro domestico originario, configurando un'immagine contemporanea e di grande comfort. Liberato lo spazio dai vecchi tavolati, lasciati a nudo i soli pilastri e le travi del soffitto, la soluzione planimetrica ha sviluppato in un lungo spazio unitario, scandito da diversi episodi compositivi, tutta la zona giorno della casa, proiettando l'interno domestico verso la vista del parco. L'ingresso si affaccia sulla sala da pranzo, delimitata virtualmente dal pilastro e dalle travi a vista del soffitto, mentre sulla sinistra, direttamente affacciato su Central Park, è organizzato il luminoso soggiorno affiancato dallo studio, nascosto da una quinta scorrevole e da un setto impiegato come ripostiglio. A scandire lo spazio unitario, che ospita soggiorno e sala da pranzo, un volume in curva rivestito in lastre di travertino quadrate si pone come efficace episodio figurativo, organizzando al suo interno la cabina armadio della zona notte. La regolare geometria del rivestimento lapideo è assunta come grammatica di riferimento per essere ripetuta in legno come riuscita conclusione della parete attrezzata dello studio, come calda superficie alle spalle del letto padronale, come motivo figurativo dei mobili contenitori che caratterizzano tutto il fronte davanti alla sala da pranzo sino alla cucina, affiancata da una camera da letto con bagno indipendente. Questa successione di raffinate superfici architettoniche caratterizza l'immagine dell'appartamento, sottolineando percorsi e prospettive interne, calibrando con attenzione gli spazi e riuscendo a concludere dal punto di vista compositivo la figura delle stanze della parte più privata della casa (studio e camera da letto padronale). Grande attenzione è stata rivolta anche all'uso dei materiali (legno chiaro per il pavimento e preziosi mosaici di marmo nel bagno) e alla figura degli arredi. Alcuni dei quali su disegno, come la consolle-scrivania in curva, con gambe di acciaio e piano di legno, nello studio o come i mobili delle camere da letto. Tutti parte di una regia globale, per uno spazio pensato in tutte le sue componenti.

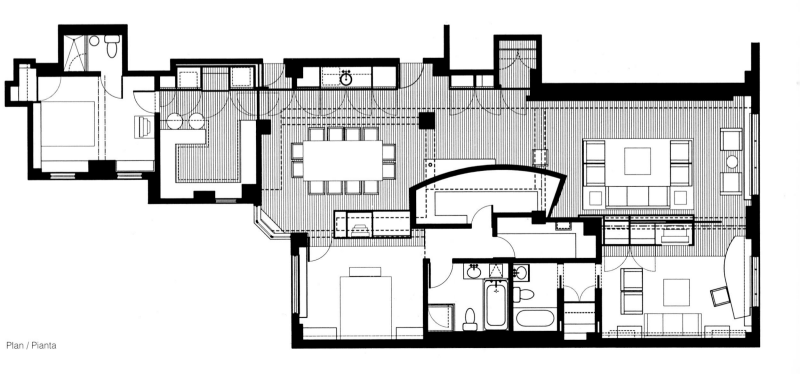

Plan / Pianta

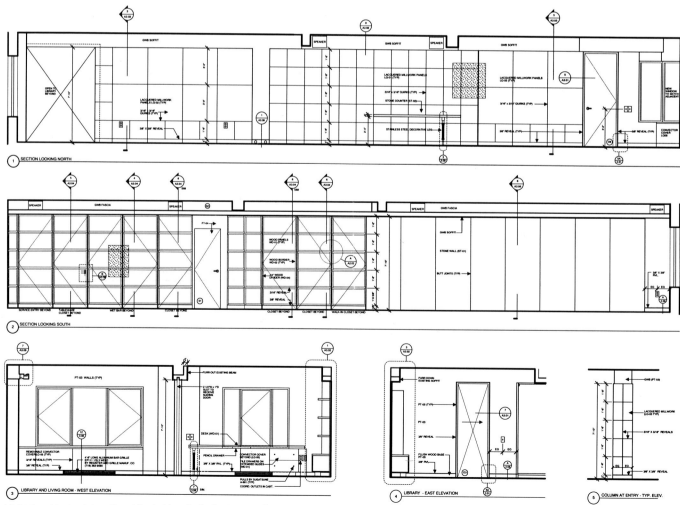

1 SECTION LOOKING NORTH

2 SECTION LOOKING SOUTH

3 LIBRARY AND LIVING ROOM - WEST ELEVATION

4 LIBRARY - EAST ELEVATION

5 COLUMN AT ENTRY - TYP. ELEV.

Vertical and horizontal sections / Sezioni longitudinali e trasversali

SPAZI VESTITI
DRESSED SPACES
Benjamin Noriega-Ortiz Architect, 1996

In restructuring this apartment, the designer was able to combine the compositional and formal, as well as the decorative and functional elements determined by the professional and personal needs of its owner, a fashion designer. The project reflects a process of synergy that constitutes a convergence between attention to arrangement and the plastic compositions and the furnishing style used in recreating the living spaces. It is an unusual blend of design and refined decor, of a selection of furniture, fabrics and coverings that "dress" the living spaces. The layout and passages optimize the natural light and the panoramic views of the city, the latter functioning as reference points. The spaces were seen as 'neutral', bright zones with well-delineated surfaces, to be characterized by furnishings, which, at times, can be transformed into architectural elements. A perfect example is the low wall, covered in gray-green fabric, which frames the two white armchairs in the living room, emphasizing the horizontal beam that crosses the entire apartment, unifying the terrace, the living room, the entrance and the dining room. This series of spaces opens onto the night zone on one side and onto the kitchen and guest room, which were built behind the dining room, on the other. A study and a bathroom are located next to the living room. The night area, which faces the entrance, is divided into two separate sections, the children's bedroom and the master bedroom. The latter, comprised of a closet and a large bathroom, covered in light stone, optimizes the corner window that frames the Chrysler and Empire State buildings. Particular attention has been given to the furnishings and the overall compositional elements, such as the fabrics selected to "dress" the chairs in the dining room and the couches in the living room, which are flanked by a sliding door-panel, separating the study, which has been redressed in a colorful pyramid pattern. The various unusual objects and furnishings, combined with the mirrors, which are used throughout the apartment, and whose gold frames afford them an antique look, accentuate the highly personalized atmosphere and comfort of this living space.

Nel ristrutturare questo grande appartamento per uno stilista di moda, il progettista è riuscito a rapportare le scelte compositive e formali, decorative e funzionali d'insieme alla professione e alla sensibilità del committente. Un'insolita miscela tra dimensione progettuale e raffinata decorazione, tra soluzione d'arredo, scelta dei tessuti e dei rivestimenti, permette di leggere il progetto di architettura d'interni come processo sinergico dove convergono attenzioni distributive e plastico-volumetriche insieme a un disegno degli arredi pensati come elementi capaci di 'vestire' gli spazi da abitare. Le scelte distributive sottolineano, nella chiarezza d'impianto e dei percorsi, la valorizzazione della luce naturale e delle viste panoramiche sulla città quali elementi di

riferimento. La scatola architettonica è assunta come spazio 'neutro' e luminoso con superfici chiare da caratterizzare con gli arredi che, a volte, si trasformano in elementi architettonici, come il muretto basso rivestito di tessuto grigio-verde che accoglie le due poltrone bianche del soggiorno e scandisce l'asse orizzontale che attraversa tutto l'appartamento, collegando in un'unica lunga prospettiva terrazza e soggiorno, ingresso e sala da pranzo. Lungo questa serie di spazi si affaccia da un lato la zona notte, dall'altro la cucina e la camera ospiti, ricavate alle spalle della sala da pranzo; uno studio con bagno autonomo si affianca poi al soggiorno. La zona notte di fronte all'ingresso è divisa in due sezioni indipendenti: la camera dei bambini e la camera da letto padronale. Questa sfrutta al meglio l'ampia finestra ad angolo che incornicia il Chrysler e l'Empire Buildings, ed è corredata da cabina armadio e da un ampio bagno rivestito di pietra chiara, particolarmente curato nell'arredo e nelle soluzioni compositive. L'arredo della zona giorno valorizza l'impiego dei tessuti, come nelle sedie 'vestite' della sala da pranzo e nei divani del soggiorno, affiancati da una porta scorrevole rivettata con borchie cromate piramidali che separa dallo studio. Grandi specchi invecchiati con cornici dorate sono distribuiti in vari punti della casa insieme a oggetti e arredi d'eccezione, per porre l'accento su un'atmosfera e un comfort di forte personalità.

136

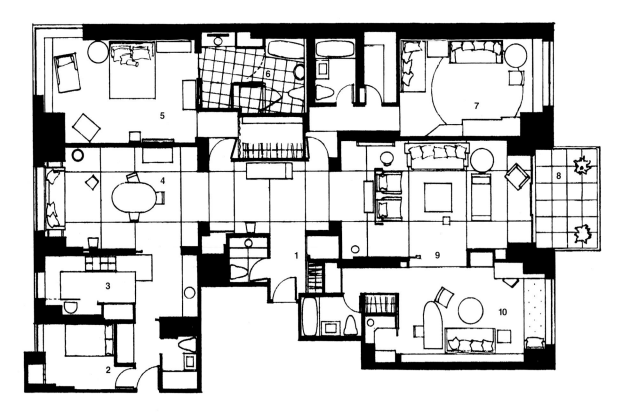

Plan / Pianta
1 . Entrance / Ingresso
2 . Guest Bedroom / Camera da letto ospiti
3 . Kitchen / Cucina
4 . Dining Room / Sala da pranzo
5 . Master Bedroom / Camera da letto padronale
6 . Master Bathroom / Bagno padronale
7 . Children's Bedroom / Camera da letto dei bambini
8 . Balcony / Balcone
9 . Living Room / Soggiorno
10. Study / Studiolo

LA CASA DEL COLLEZIONISTA
THE COLLECTOR'S HOME
Parson + Fernandez-Casteleiro Architects PC, 1993

This luxurious and traditional apartment was transformed into an unusual home for a collector of ancient art, who chose to convert his home into a sort of private museum. The project has radically altered the apartment, creating spaces that are more similar to those of a museum or art exhibit than to those of a traditional home. The changes have gone so far as to alter the denomination of rooms that function as the bedroom or the living or the dining room. These rooms have been given names such as the "White Room", the "Conversation Room" and the "Library". The shapes and materials used to decorate these autonomous spaces are also used to fulfil the domestic functions that are typically associated with these rooms. The layout corresponds to a compositional style, which, in response to the expositional needs, brilliantly leaves an imprint, provoking a series of alterations and desired juxtapositions. The result is an increased dialectical proximity to the "historical" tracks, reminiscent of the house's original decorative and structural style. In the dark green vestibule, a complex apparatus floats in the small space, announcing the strong, personal character of the house. A central hallway-gallery, with a dark gray pavement and linear steel panels (a solution used throughout the apartment), is flanked by the "White Room", dedicated to the exposition of Roman statues. The hallway continues into the conversation room, which is characterized by a bronze torso. This is also where the terracotta pieces are displayed. Here, below a vault, an intricate system comprised of draped, double curtains allows the natural light to be electronically controlled, altering the internal ambience. The library also functions as an additional museum piece, with its perforated aluminum panels, which cover the windows that function as supports for the paintings. The latter are illuminated through the use of a specially designed lighting system. A glass platform rests on transparent plastic disks, which are affixed to metal pegs, supporting two movable day beds, which have been converted into comfortable reading sofas. The cantilevered slate top desk in the corner of the room provides the final expression of the decor's planned mechanics.

138

Un lussuoso e tradizionale appartamento è stato trasformato in un'inconsueta abitazione per un collezionista di arte antica, che ha scelto di fare della propria casa una sorta di museo privato. In effetti il progetto ha cambiato radicalmente il senso di tutti gli ambienti, avvicinandoli più alla categoria di spazi museali o di allestimenti d'arte che a quella di tradizionali luoghi domestici. Anzitutto, le funzioni di camera da letto, soggiorno, sala da pranzo sono state abbandonate in favore di categorie astratte quali "Camera Bianca", "Camera di conversazione" e "Libreria", luoghi autonomi, di diversa figura e materiale, che secondo le esigenze possono essere anche utilizzati per le consuete funzioni domestiche. Alla chiarezza dell'impianto risponde una dirompente grammatica compositiva che, rispondendo in modo brillante alle esigenze espositive, aggiunge segni e soluzioni progettuali che provocano una serie di studiati slittamenti e di voluti contrappunti, per affiancarsi in modo dialettico alle tracce 'storiche' (modanature e infissi lignei) che ricordano l'immagine originaria della casa. Nel vestibolo, colorato di verde scuro, una complessa installazione fluttua nel piccolo spazio annunciando il forte e personale carattere della casa.

Un corridoio-galleria centrale, con pavimento in sisal grigio scuro e pannelli di acciaio in linea (soluzione ripetuta in tutto l'appartamento), è affiancata dalla "Camera Bianca", dedicata all'esposizione delle statue romane, per concludersi nella grande stanza di conversazione, segnata da un torso di bronzo, dove sono organizzate le terrecotte. Qui, sotto una volta di gesso, un sistema di doppie tende elettrificate a drappeggio permette di dosare la luce naturale e di cambiare l'atmosfera interna. La biblioteca si configura come ulteriore ambiente museale, caratterizzato dai pannelli in lamiera forata che coprono le finestre di facciata per sostenere i quadri illuminati con uno studiato sistema di luci su disegno. Una piattaforma di vetro, poggiante su dischi in materiale plastico trasparente fissati su perni metallici, sostiene due letti da ospedale trasformati in confortevoli divani da lettura spostabili su binario. La ricercata macchinolatria dell'arredo, trova nella scrivania dell'angolo studio un'efficace conclusione espressiva.

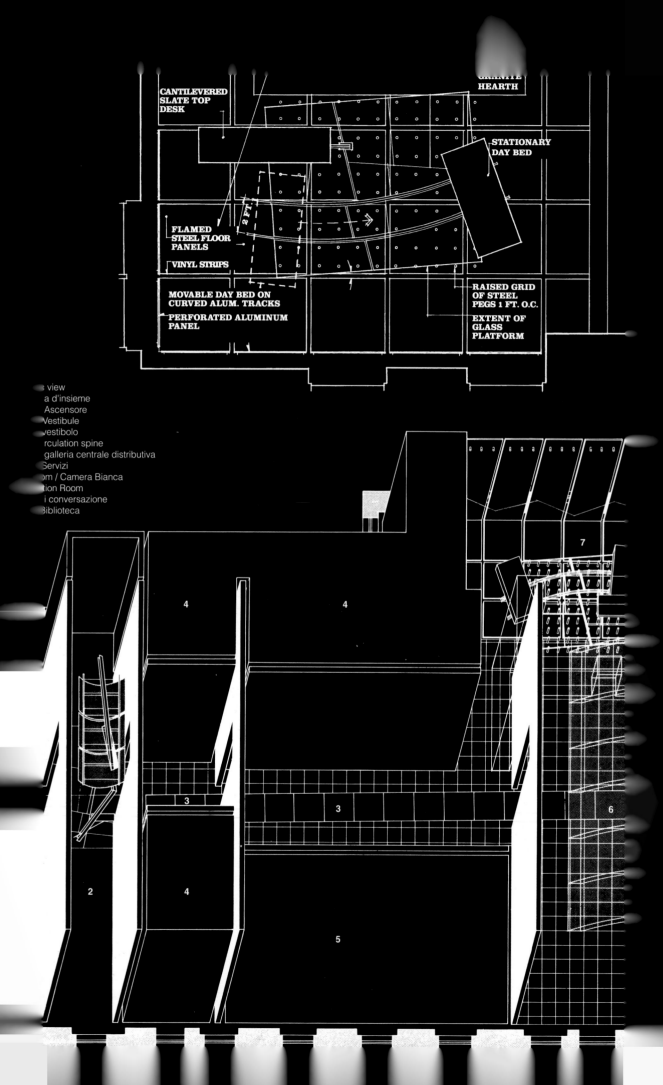

CANTILEVERED SLATE TOP DESK

GRANITE HEARTH

STATIONARY DAY BED

FLAMED STEEL FLOOR PANELS

2 FT.

VINYL STRIPS

MOVABLE DAY BED ON CURVED ALUM. TRACKS

PERFORATED ALUMINUM PANEL

RAISED GRID OF STEEL PEGS 1 FT. O.C.

EXTENT OF GLASS PLATFORM

2

4

4

3

3

4

5

7

6

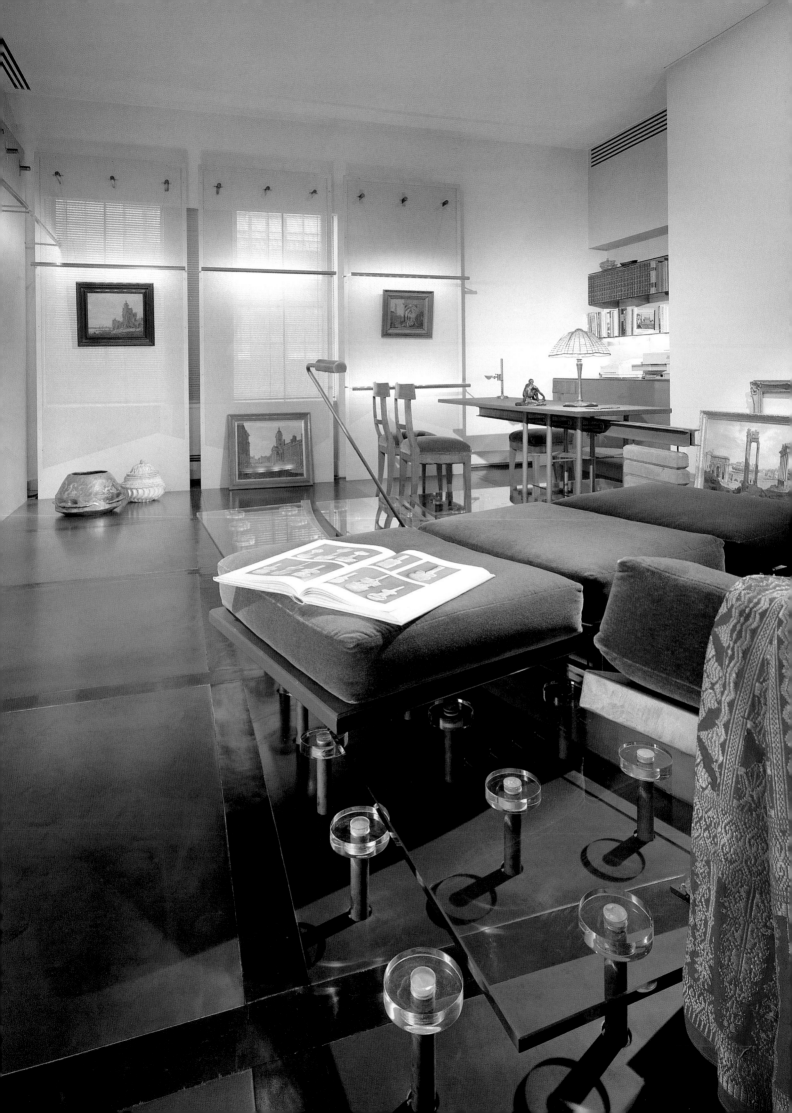

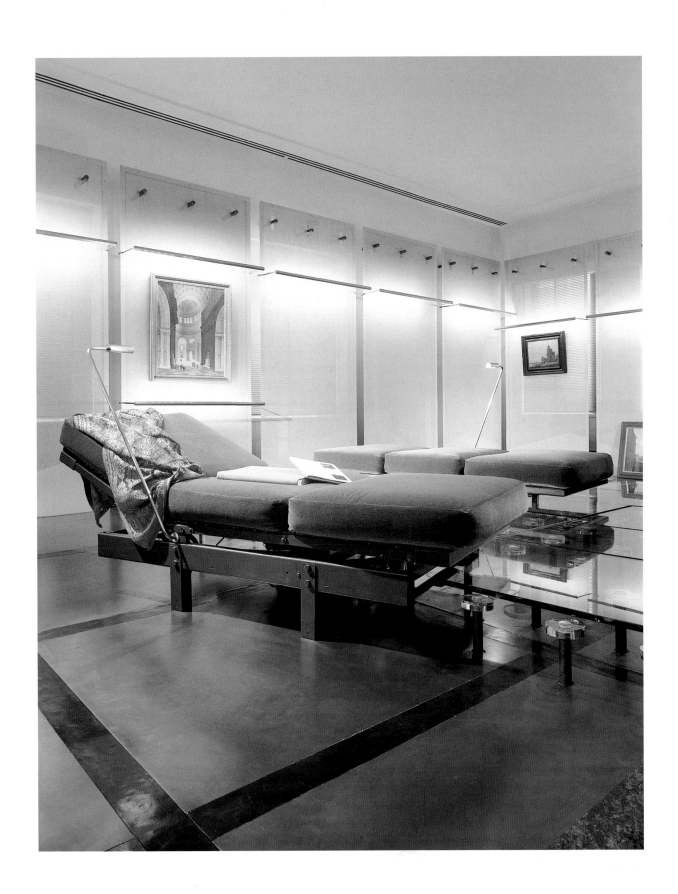

DETTAGLIO E IRONIA
DETAIL AND IRONY
Marco Pasanella, 1996

In restructuring, or, better, in "characterizing" his own home, Marco Pasanella, journalist, photographer and founder of a multidisciplinary design studio, engraved his personality and ironic humor. Divided in the traditional manner, with the living room/dining room and bedroom located along the main façade, and the storage room, bathroom and kitchen at the back, the apartment did not require radical alterations; rather, it necessitated a slight reinterpretation. Hence, its eighteenth century character was left intact, with its colored walls and thick reliefs and white-washed wooden doors, stuccoes and the cozy parquet. With the aim of creating a living environment "to be rediscovered daily" (Pasanella), the changes focused on the objects, their shape and their arrangement, which, at times, seems almost 'Dadaist'. The wooden stairway in the living room, for example, reaches up to a ledge that rests almost at ceiling height, or the kitchen table with its black marble surface into which cutlery and dishes have been drawn and engraved in white marble, providing the impression of a set table. It is a creative and ironic image born of an almost maniacal taste for detail, which is repeated again and again in all the rooms, without, however, appearing forced or overdone. In this manner, small and slight inventions, created by making balanced changes, are tastefully alternated according to a tightly planned design. In the living room, an old tripod forms the base for a long natural wood plank that seems to be on the verge of falling. The ledge of the white-washed fireplace displays a trophy stone, which consists of a small red, stuffed fish. In the entrance, two "plain", custom-made twin tables are transformed into flower vases and photo frames. The towels in the bathroom are embroidered with the words "bath", "face" and "hands", ironically stating their purposes. In the bedroom, an old wall safe is used as an unusual storage space. The bed is designed to resemble a small castle, with four thin towers, each one differing in height, extending the supports of the bed's legs. Finally, an embroidered oval hole in the curtain becomes a lookout point, enabling the viewer to observe the outside, without, however, being watched.

Nel ristrutturare, o meglio nel 'caratterizzare', la propria abitazione Marco Pasanella, giornalista e fotografo, fondatore di uno studio di design multidisciplinare, ha tradotto in chiave domestica la sua personalità e la propria ironia. Diviso in modo tradizionale, con soggiorno-pranzo e camera da letto lungo la facciata principale, ripostigli, bagno e cucina sul retro, il piccolo appartamento non richiedeva interventi radicali, quanto piuttosto una sottile e leggera rinterpretazione. Così il carattere ottocentesco della casa è rimasto invariato con colori tenui alle pareti, spesse modanature e porte in legno dipinte di bianco, stucchi e un caldo parquet. Ciò che è cambiato, nel riuscito tentativo di creare uno spazio domestico "da scoprire ogni volta che si torna a casa" (Pasanella), è il senso degli oggetti, la loro figura e il loro posizionamento, a volte quasi 'dadaista' come per la scala a pioli di legno che nel soggiorno raggiunge una mensola posta quasi all'altezza del soffitto, o come il tavolo della cucina con piano di marmo nero dove sono disegnati e inseriti, in marmo bianco, posate e piatti di una stilizzata tavola apparecchiata. Un gioco ironico e creativo, un gusto quasi maniacale per i dettagli, si ripete stanza per stanza, senza mai apparire troppo disegnato o forzatamente compositivo. Così una serie di piccole e leggere invenzioni, dei calibrati slittamenti, si alternano con garbo, secondo una studiata regia. Nel soggiorno un vecchio cavalletto a tre piedi in ghisa è la base per un lungo piano di legno naturale che sembra in bilico, quasi per cadere. Il caminetto tinteggiato di bianco, sostiene sulla sua mensola di pietra un trofeo costituito da un piccolo pesce rosso impagliato. Nell'ingresso due 'semplici' tavolini gemelli su disegno si trasformano in portafiori e in portafoto. Gli asciugamani nel bagno sono ricamati con le scritte "bagno", "faccia", "mani", sottolineando ironicamente le loro funzioni. Nella camera da letto una vecchia cassaforte a muro funge da inconsueta mensola-ripostiglio. Il letto è pensato come un piccolo castello con quattro torri sottili di diversa altezza che prolungano i sostegni delle gambe. Infine nella tenda un buco ovale ricamato diventa un oblò per guardare il paesaggio esterno, senza però essere osservati.

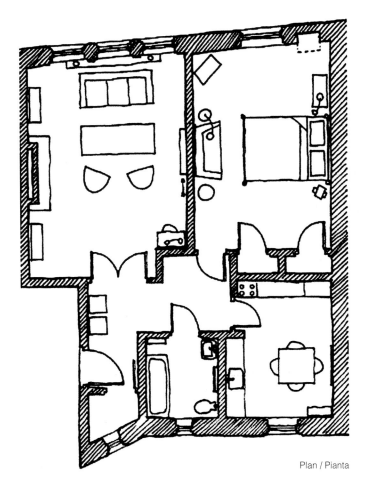

Plan / Pianta

EXPOSITIONAL ELEGANCE

Pasanella, Klein Stolzman, Berg, Architects PC, 1993

This refined apartment, located in a luxurious building on Fifth Avenue that overlooks Central Park, was restructured, balancing living space and an exposition gallery. The result is a functional arrangement whose central hallway houses a modern art collection and an exhibit of African sculptures, within a warm and comfortable home environment. Two bedrooms have been placed in the interior of the living space, while the kitchen and multifunctional room/study are at the center. The large living room, adjoined to the dining room, is located along the façade that overlooks the park, as are the master bedroom, a detached bathroom and a walk-in closet that leads to the study in front of the kitchen. Particular attention has been given to the selection of materials and to the careful design of niches and exposition areas for the artwork, which is arranged throughout the house. These spaces are created with such good taste and discretion that they do not conflict with the more domestic and private elements of the apartment. With the exception of the kitchen, the floors are covered in mahogany and embellished by large carpets. Immense, natural wood panels cover a vast portion of the walls, alternating with darker niches that house some of the collection's pieces. The kitchen's composition harmonizes with the elegance of the apartment's decor. Its illuminated suspensions are like a set of bright windows and the parquet's motif resembles an abstract painting. The composition and the blend of various vertical surfaces (wood panels flanked by white walls, airy, glazed windows used as a background frame for sculptures and sliding doors of silk and steel that separate the living room from the dining room), are exalted by the central image of the specially designed fireplace, made of large, full-height, marble slabs, interrupted by a light ledge, made of the same material. The furniture serves to emphasize the warmth and extreme comfort of this refined interior design. Some of the custom-made furniture includes the sofas under the windows, a privileged viewpoint from which to observe the city and the park.

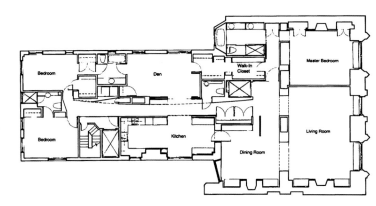

Plan / Pianta

In uno dei lussuosi edifici residenziali affacciati dalla Fifth Avenue su Central Park è stato ristrutturato questo raffinato appartamento. Un calibrato spazio domestico, studiato per organizzare un'importante collezione d'arte moderna e di sculture africane all'interno di una nuova funzionale distribuzione e di un caldo comfort. La soluzione planimetrica di progetto ha trasformato il corridoio centrale in galleria espositiva per quadri e sculture, organizzando due camere da letto verso l'interno, cucina e stanza-studio polivalente al centro, l'ampio soggiorno collegato alla sala da pranzo lungo il fronte affacciato sul parco, così come la camera da letto padronale, corredata di bagno indipendente e di cabina armadio passante verso la camera-studio di fronte alla cucina. Particolare attenzione è stata rivolta alla scelta dei materiali e alla studiata creazione di nicchie e zone espositive per i pezzi d'arte che sono così disposti con garbo e discrezione in tutte le zone della casa, senza incombere sul carattere domestico e privato degli spazi. Un parquet di mogano copre, ad esclusione della cucina, tutta la superficie dell'appartamento arricchito da grandi tappeti; ampie pannellature di legno naturale nascondono parte delle pareti, alternandosi a nicchie più scure che accolgono alcuni pezzi della collezione. La cucina, con pensili illuminati come serie di luminose finestre, presenta un particolare parquet in diverse essenze, posato secondo un motivo che simula una sorta di quadro astratto, in sintonia con l'eleganza dell'intero progetto. La composizione e l'incastro tra diverse superfici verticali (pannelli di legno affiancati ai muri bianchi, leggere vetrate acidate impiegate come sfondo per incorniciare alcune sculture, porte scorrevoli di seta e acciaio per separare soggiorno da sala da pranzo) sono sottolineati anche nell'essenziale figura del camino centrale su disegno, formato da ampie lastre marmoree a tutt'altezza interrotte da una leggera mensola aggettante dello stesso materiale. L'arredo vuole sottolineare il calore e l'alto comfort di questo raffinato progetto d'interni. Tra i pezzi su disegno si notano i divanetti fissi posti sotto le finestre affacciate sul parco; postazioni privilegiate per osservare la città.

ABITARE CON L'ARTE
LIVING WITH ART
Pasanella, Klein Stolzman, Berg, Architects PC, 1989

The project's primary objective was to fulfil the owner's need to expose her art collection; however, unable to convert a home into an art gallery, the designers followed a "trial and error" work strategy that enabled "the often bizarre art objects to maintain their position on center stage". Although the new layout tends to develop the available space longitudinally, the traditional arrangement of the apartment's separate spaces was not abandoned. The entrance hall, the project's main port of entry, is characterized by two portals covered in quadrangular zinc panels. To the right, a small study and the living room, located next to the kitchen, are separated from the entrance by two sliding doors in sandblasted glass. They are supported by an essential metallic ledge. To the left, the ample living room opens onto the raised terrace that overlooks Central Park. The night zone, located on the same level, is separated from the living room by a thick wall of panels, which are placed on cylindrical lead pegs and supported by metal cornerstones. This is a refined and practical solution for displaying art objects. The bedroom and terrace, which are connected to each other, are configured as distinct spaces, separate from the rest of the house, even in terms of the materials used in their construction. The use of light appears to be one of the project's central elements of composition. A set of small and essential beams, anchored to a raised linear support, illuminate the artwork in a flexible manner, their light acting upon the environment, altering it. The lights are placed at the height of a metal shade, which, inconspicuously, but powerfully, characterizes the entire parameter of the house, with the exception of the zinc panels. The metallic, horizontal line appears to outline the terrace's essential ledges, but it also crowns the kitchen furniture and, finally, it serves as a sash, enveloping the upper portion of the bathroom's tiled surface. This apartment is a unique compositional synthesis that is able to create a harmonious accord between living space and an exposition gallery, emphasizing both the image and the contents.

Il progetto doveva anzitutto rispondere all'esigenza di mostrare al meglio la collezione d'arte della proprietaria, ma, gli autori non potendo trasformare una casa in una galleria espositiva, hanno lavorato seguendo una strategia di riduzione basata su "tentativi ed errori", in grado "di fare rimanere gli oggetti d'arte, a volte bizzarri, al centro del palcoscenico". La tradizionale distribuzione ad ambienti separati della casa non è stata abbandonata, nonostante le soluzioni di progetto tendano a fare emergere lo sviluppo longitudinale degli spazi. Un foyer d'ingresso, segnato da due portali rivestiti con pannelli quadrangolari di zinco rivettati, si pone come cerniera spaziale dell'intero intervento. Sulla destra si accede a un piccolo studio e alla sala da pranzo accanto alla cucina, entrambi separati dall'ingresso con due porte scorrevoli di vetro sabbiato sostenuto da un essenziale infisso metallico. Sulla sinistra si apre l'ampio soggiorno proiettato verso la terrazza affacciata su Central Park. La zona notte, rialzata come la terrazza rispetto alla quota d'ingresso, è divisa dal soggiorno con una forte parete di lastre di calcare poggianti su perni cilindrici di piombo e sostenute da angolari di metallo; raffinato e riuscito fondale per disporre oggetti d'arte. Camera da letto e terrazza, tra loro collegate, si definiscono come spazi distinti, zone compiute separate dal resto della casa anche dal punto di vista materico. L'uso della luce appare nel progetto uno degli elementi di riferimento: essenziali e leggeri faretti in serie ancorati a un supporto lineare a sbalzo illuminano i pezzi d'arte in modo flessibile, animando il soggiorno secondo le necessità. Le luci sono poste all'altezza di uno scuretto metallico che segna in modo silenzioso, ma deciso, tutto il perimetro della casa ad eccezione delle lastre di calcare. La linea metallica orizzontale compare in altro modo a segnare gli essenziali infissi della terrazza, nella cucina come coronamento dei mobili e infine come fascia superiore della superficie piastrellata dei bagni. Una sintesi compositiva capace di fare di un'abitazione anche uno spazio che, con singolare armonia, accoglie una collezione d'arte valorizzandone immagine e contenuto

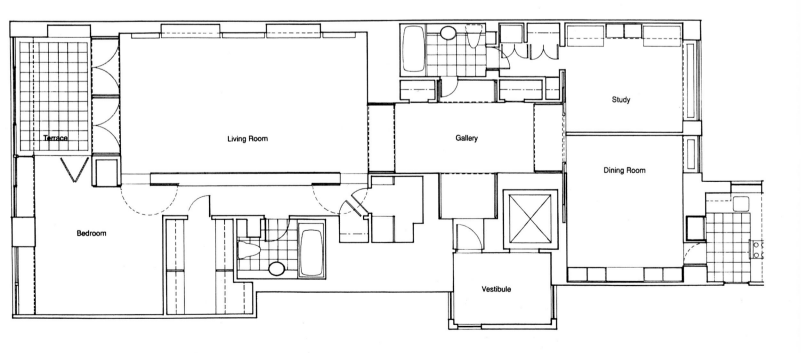

Plan / Pianta

CENTRAL PARK WEST
CENTRAL PARK WEST

Lee Harris Pomeroy Architects, 1996

In one of the luxurious and monumental buildings of Central Park West, an area that has always been known for its exclusive residences, two apartments were connected to create a single, immense living space. The restructuring project completely transformed the spaces in terms of both, materials and internal decor. The new layout, intended to optimize the urban view of Central Park, is the result of a complete redesigning of the internal sections. The front part of the house has been created as an open-space, taking advantage of the natural light and the views offered by the windowed façade. Here, the material used for the parquet unifies the entrance (with horizontally positioned light marble inserts) with the dining room and the large living room. These rooms are characterized by a set of custom-made, full-height bookshelves in mahogany, which strongly emphasize and balance the carefully orchestrated succession of their uses. Sliding and rotating vertical, wood surfaces, placed on central pegs, flank doors that permit the day area to be separated from the kitchen, built in light wood, and the succession of rooms, built along the long corridor, that are used for free time activities (game room, gym, a study). Some of the custom-made furniture (B-Five Studio) follows the traditional style of comfort provided by the Thirties and Art Déco, while others do not compromise their modernity. The night zone, with its private entrance, is located on the right and is designed to function as an independent living area. Here, the new layout follows the refined sensibility used in the original arrangement of these buildings, which features large rooms located in a series along the central hallway. The corner in which the master bedroom is located is particularly well designed. It is separated from the circular, corner study by a vanishing sliding door. The bright master bathroom is covered in Botticino marble, providing an elegant synthesis of essential geometrical shapes. A second kitchen, left standing from the original layout, accesses the children's bedrooms and the service area.

In uno dei lussuosi edifici monumentali di Central Park West, da sempre sede di esclusive residenze, sono stati uniti due appartamenti per formare un'unica grande unità abitativa, completamente trasformata sia dal punto di vista distributivo, sia da quello dei materiali e delle figure d'interni. La nuova disposizione planimetrica, definita per valorizzare al meglio la scena urbana di Central Park, è frutto di un ridisegno completo delle partizioni interne. Una prima zona della casa è stata pensata come spazio aperto, che sfrutta al meglio la luce naturale e le viste offerte dal fronte finestrato. Qui un caldo pavimento di parquet unifica a livello materico gli spazi dell'ingresso (con inserti di marmo chiaro disposti a conci orizzontali), della sala da pranzo e dell'ampio soggiorno, scanditi da una serie di mobili libreria su disegno in mogano che, in posizione centrale e a tutt'altezza, segnano fortemente e calibrano con studiata regia la successione delle diverse funzioni. Superfici verticali in legno, scorrevoli e girevoli su perno centrale, si affiancano alle porte per separare, se necessario, la zona giorno dalla cucina abitabile in legno chiaro e dalla successione di spazi per il tempo libero (stanza per i giochi, la ginnastica, uno studio) disposti lungo un corridoio attrezzato. Alcuni arredi su disegno (B-Five Studio) rileggono la tradizione del comfort domestico del periodo anni Trenta e Art Déco, altri non rinunciano alla loro modernità. La zona notte, con ingresso indipendente, si sviluppa sulla destra come sezione abitativa autonoma. Qui la soluzione planimetrica di progetto ricorda con raffinata sensibilità la tradizionale distribuzione storica propria di questi edifici, con ampie stanze poste in serie lungo il corridoio centrale. Particolarmente riuscito l'angolo occupato dalla camera da letto padronale, divisa dallo studiolo circolare d'angolo con una porta scorrevole in curva a scomparsa. Il luminoso bagno padronale rivestito in Botticino si propone come elegante sintesi di essenziali geometrie. Una seconda cucina preesistente anticipa le altre camere da letto per i bambini e la zona di servizio.

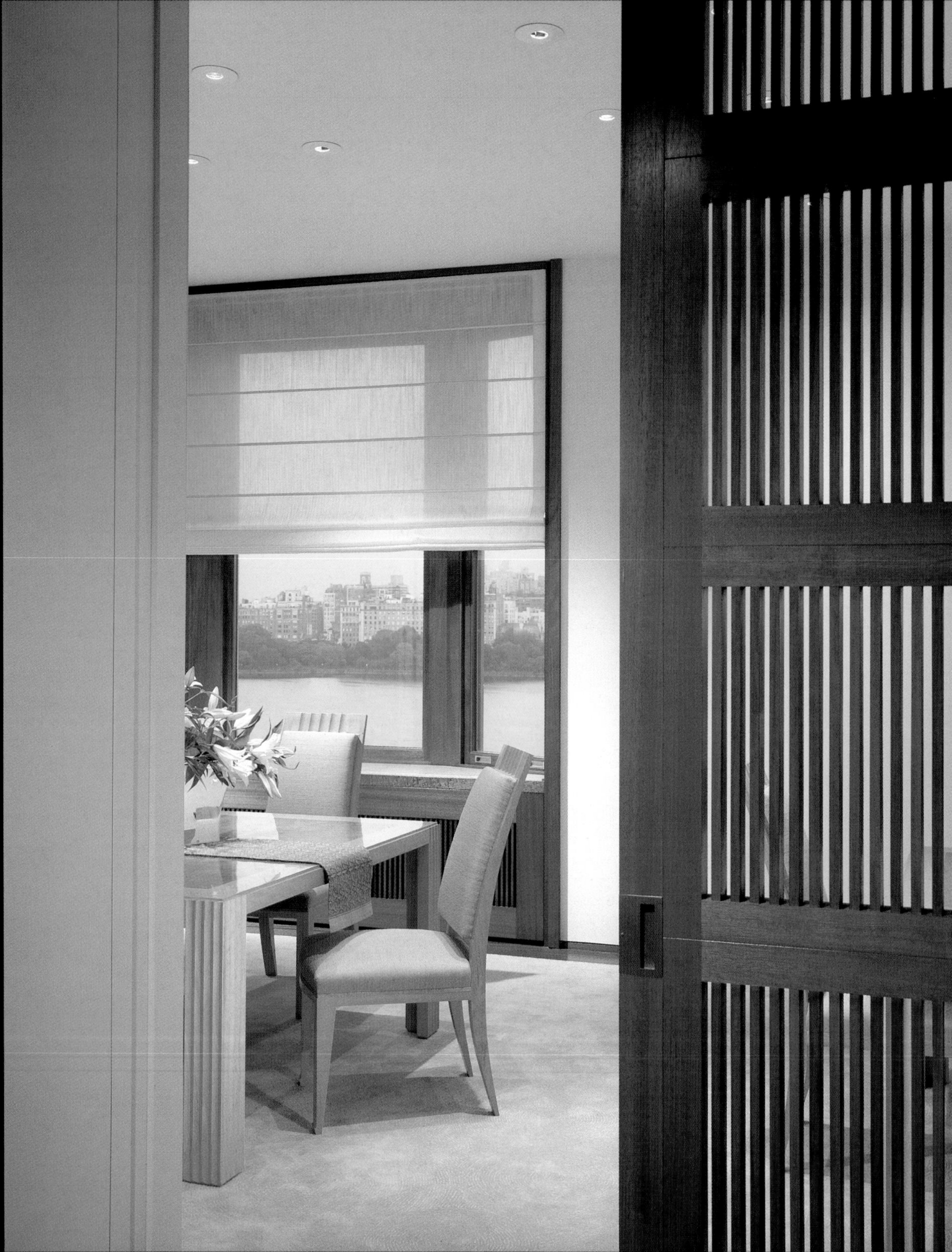

179

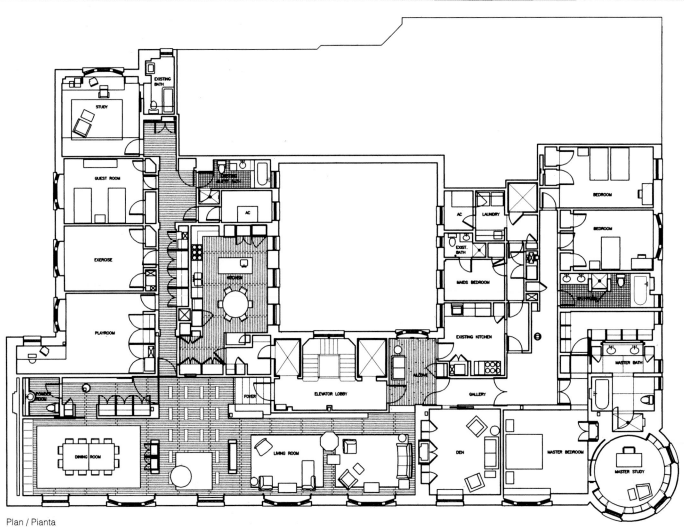

Plan / Pianta

COLORI FORTI
STRONG COLORS
Peter Stamberg & Paul Aferiat Architects, 1988

At times, the restructuring of a domestic environment must respect a limited budget, while contemporaneously preserving the original structure as much as possible. This must be done, however, without having to renounce the creation of a new image, which can radically change a space's significance. The philosophy of this particular project involved an approach based on the concept of working with what is available and making small additions, introducing new materials and making clear cut changes in color. The architectural shell was, therefore, recreated, using dark colors to give the walls an independent character, optimizing the similarities and contrasts in shades. The bright hues (yellow, green and hot pink) were able to transform the apartment's image and atmosphere without altering the size, the pavements, the ceilings with horizontal beams, the reliefs and the ledges. Some elements were the subject of slight alterations, such as the classical fireplace in the living room, whose opening was reduced to a stone insert; a solution also used in the pavement as protection against sparks. Some of the rooms in the house were resized and reconstructed. The bright bathroom, for example, originally characterized by a detailed pattern, was covered with light gray tiles. The new color was enlivened by the addition of natural wood furniture, arranged according to their varying depths. The hanging mirrors and the L-shaped, steel counter, in which the semi-circular sink is placed, provided an additional effect. Careful attention to design and to the selection of furniture is obvious throughout the house. Even the well-planned arrangement of artwork contributes to the comfort and personal flare given to the apartment. The entire composition is based on an interplay of colors, from the custom-made furniture, such as the glass table with different colored legs found in the dining room and surrounded by a vivid assortment of colored chairs in wood (the famous series 7 by Arne Jacobsen, 1955), to the newly selected furniture (among which, the Philippe Starck armchairs), to the lively cushions on the sofas.

A volte la rinconfigurazione di un interno domestico deve essere condotta con un budget ridotto, cercando di conservare quanto più è possibile della struttura esistente, senza tuttavia rinunciare a definire una nuova immagine in grado di cambiare radicalmente il senso di uno spazio. È il caso di questo intervento dove la filosofia di approccio progettuale può essere sintetizzata nel concetto di lavorare sull'esistente, attraverso leggere aggiunte, nuovi materiali e decisi slittamenti cromatici. L'involucro architettonico è stato così riqualificato con uno studio dei colori pensati per caratterizzare le pareti come superfici indipendenti, valorizzate nell'accostamento e nel confronto. L'accesa palette delle tinte (giallo, verde e rosa squillanti) è riuscita a trasformare la figura e l'atmosfera dell'appartamento nonostante dimensioni, pavimenti e soffitti a travi orizzontali, modanature e infissi, siano sostanzialmente rimasti immutati. Alcuni elementi sono

stati oggetto di leggere alterazioni, come il caminetto classico del soggiorno, la cui apertura è stata ridotta con un inserto di pietra, ripetuto anche sul pavimento come elemento di protezione dalle scintille. Alcune stanze della casa sono state ridimensionate e ricostruite, come il luminoso bagno caratterizzato dalla cura del disegno complessivo: il rivestimento di piastrelle grigio chiaro è interrotto dai mobili di legno naturale disposti secondo diverse profondità, cui si aggiungono i pensili a specchio e il piano di acciaio a 'L' continuo dove si incastra il lavabo semisferico. Una forte attenzione verso il disegno e la selezione degli arredi si esprime in tutte le zone della casa; anche la studiata presenza di opere d'arte contribuisce a definire il comfort e la personalità dell'abitazione. Dai mobili su disegno, come il tavolo dal piano in vetro con gambe in diversi colori della sala da pranzo, circondato da una divertita gamma cromatica di sedie in compensato curvato (la famosa series 7 di Arne Jacobsen del 1955), a quelli selezionati in produzione (tra cui le poltroncine di Philippe Starck), ai vivaci cuscini dei divani, tutto si rapporta alla tensione d'insieme, giocata sulla composizione di colori forti.

193

SCULPTURED WALL

Peter Stamberg & Paul Aferiat Architects, 1990

This domestic interior, designed for a couple of fashion designers, is characterized by a vibrant choice of colors, as well as by its compositional creativity, which found a way of connecting the entrance with the living room. The internal layout has maintained its original structure, with the day zone and the bedroom clearly separated from each other, the latter being an independent space with its own adjoining bathroom. The overall architectural layout, however, has undergone radical restructuring. The addition of a second bathroom was a functional necessity. Located between the entrance and the dining room, it has been transformed into a bright yellow, compositional element that functions as a connective entry to the foyer, which overlooks the large living room. The other compositional element of reference is the light green sculpted wall. It begins at the entrance and extends to the new bathroom, placed in a curve, to then rotate, moving along the blind wall of the living room, terminating at a new paneled fireplace. The succession of niches and figurative elements configured by this strong architectural design constitute an efficient solution that is able to provide a single pathway from entrance to foyer to living room. The green wall, which was kept detached from the ceiling to allow an efficient indirect embedded light to be installed, is a compositional element with horizontal cuts that are alternated with niches that house flower vases, artwork and sculptures. These include a reproduction of the Venus by Milo, painted in electric blue, a gift from the designer Yves Klein. In addition to the new walls, another important change is represented by the design of the furnishings, complemented by a selection of signed works by Monique and Sergio Savarese for Dialogica. The shape and color schemes of the furniture are designated by the overall image. Chairs and sofas are arranged in a manner that guides the view and perspective of the interior. The red "Cardinal dotts" chair by Peter Stamberg, for example, is strategically positioned in front of the entrance, while the ledge of the paneled fireplace, houses a curious collection of miniature models of columns and obelisks.

Questa riqualificazione di un interno domestico disegnato per una coppia di stilisti, si caratterizza per una squillante scelta cromatica e per l'invenzione compositiva di connessione tra ingresso e soggiorno. La distribuzione interna è stata mantenuta come nella situazione preesistente, con una netta separazione tra zona giorno e camera da letto. Questa è pensata come spazio indipendente con bagno proprio. La scatola architettonica è stata tuttavia oggetto di interventi radicali e di segno deciso. Anzitutto, dal punto di vista funzionale si è aggiunto un secondo necessario bagno di servizio, collocato tra ingresso e sala da pranzo, trasformato in elemento plastico colorato giallo acido che funge da cerniera volumetrica di connessione con il foyer affacciato sull'ampio soggiorno. L'altro elemento compositivo di riferimento è il muro scultoreo tinteggiato verde chiaro, che dall'ingresso si sviluppa di fronte al nuovo bagno in curva, per poi ruotare proseguendo lungo il fronte cieco del soggiorno e terminare con un nuovo camino di lamiera spazzolata. La successione di nicchie e di episodi figurativi definiti dal disegno di questo forte segno architettonico costituisce una riuscita soluzione in grado di proporre come unico percorso la successione ingresso-foyer-soggiorno. Il muro verde, tenuto staccato dal soffitto anche per ospitare un'efficace luce indiretta incassata, si propone come elemento compiuto, interrotto da tagli orizzontali alternati a nicchie espositive dove sono collocati vasi di fiori, opere d'arte e sculture, come una riproduzione della Venere di Milo tinta blu elettrico, omaggio dei progettisti a Yves Klein. Insieme ai nuovi segni murari, grande importanza ha avuto il disegno degli arredi, affiancati da una selezione di pezzi firmati da Monique e Sergio Savarese per Dialogica. Figura e colore dei mobili sono rapportati all'immagine d'insieme; sedie e divani sono disposti anche per risolvere e concludere viste e prospettive interne, come la sedia rossa 'Cardinal dotts" di Peter Stamberg posizionata in modo strategico di fronte all'ingresso o come il camino conclusivo di lamiera imbullonata, pensato anche per ospitare sulla mensola una curiosa collezione di modellini in bronzo di colonne e obelischi.

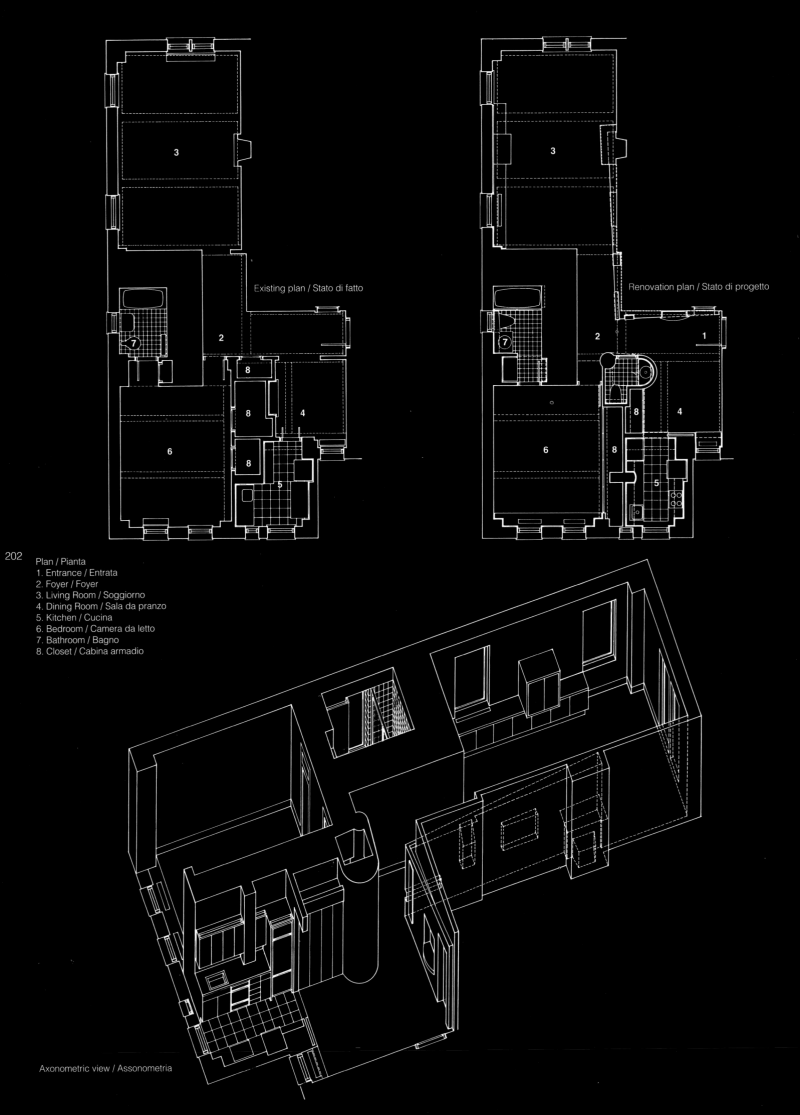

Existing plan / Stato di fatto

Renovation plan / Stato di progetto

202   Plan / Pianta
1. Entrance / Entrata
2. Foyer / Foyer
3. Living Room / Soggiorno
4. Dining Room / Sala da pranzo
5. Kitchen / Cucina
6. Bedroom / Camera da letto
7. Bathroom / Bagno
8. Closet / Cabina armadio

Axonometric view / Assonometria

PROGETTO PER PARTI
PROJECT BY PARTS
Peter Stamberg & Paul Aferiat Architects, 1991

This apartment, characterized by its view of the East River, is the result of the unification of three smaller apartments, which were connected to each other at different times. The project concerns the third apartment, which has joined two of the rooms in the original layout, creating a new, bright day zone that is directly connected to the entrance. The initial objective of the restructuring was to dynamically push the internal pathways of the internal design toward the panoramic view of the river, considered to be a fixed scene upon which to base the entire architectural design. The dark corridor, where a small cooking area had originally been placed, was completely eliminated, enabling the entire space to be unified and a new foyer to be connected to a relax room and to the study-bedroom, which completes the new architectural layout. The structural obstacles were brilliantly overcome by transforming a pillar into a cylindrical column covered in copper. The new

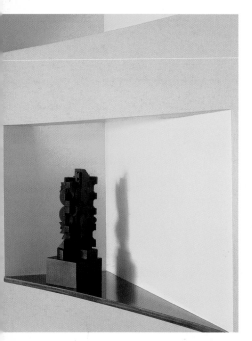

foyer, a plastic, compositional element that completes the new internal perspective, is a detailed pathway, characterized by a set of imposing episodes. Beginning with the entrance, there is a play on the exposed beams of the ceiling and the balanced embeddings that emphasize the overall compositional style. To the left, the relax area opens onto the foyer, allowing the natural light to reach even the more internal spaces. To the right, the blind wall has been transformed into an efficient display wall, marked by a set of yellow niches, which have been carefully illuminated. At the far end, behind the cylindrical column, the wall curves to direct the path toward the study, which completes the course, and to emphasize the space's tendency to turn toward the view of the river. Some of the study's fixed furnishings follow the sway of the curve of the display wall, thereby underlining the overall solution, enabling the study to be included in the unified compositional form, which begins at the entrance. Even the original bedroom has been carefully redesigned, allowing the custom-made, natural wood panel, with its copper ledges, to emerge, characterizing an entire wall with its dynamic and geometrical immensity.

Frutto della somma di tre piccoli appartamenti uniti tra loro in diverse fasi, quest'abitazione si caratterizza per la vista panoramica sull'East River. Il progetto si riferisce alla terza addizione che ha collegato due stanze all'abitazione esistente, organizzando una nuova luminosa zona giorno, direttamente collegata all'ingresso. Spunto iniziale della nuova sistemazione è stato l'obiettivo di spingere dinamicamente i percorsi interni verso la vista panoramica del fiume, assunto come scena fissa cui riferire l'intera soluzione progettuale. Il buio corridoio attrezzato dove era collocato un piccolo angolo cottura è stato completamente eliminato, riuscendo a sfruttare l'intero spazio in senso unitario e a legare il nuovo foyer a una stanza relax e allo studio-camera da letto che conclude il nuovo percorso architettonico. Superati i vincoli strutturali in modo brillante, trasformando un pilastro in una forte colonna cilindrica rivestita di rame, plastico elemento compositivo di conclusione della studiata prospettiva interna, il nuovo foyer si propone come un articolato percorso scandito da una serie di episodi rilevanti. Anzitutto dall'ingresso si coglie il gioco del soffitto con travi portanti a vista e calibrati incastri che sottolineano il gioco compositivo d'insieme. Sulla sinistra la zona relax è aperta sul foyer, permettendo alla luce naturale di arrivare anche nella zona più interna. Sulla destra il muro cieco è stato trasformato in efficace parete espositiva, segnata da una serie di nicchie colorate di giallo, illuminate con attenzione. Sul fondo, alle spalle della colonna cilindrica, la parete s'incurva per proiettare il percorso verso lo studio conclusivo e per enfatizzare la propensione dello spazio a rivolgersi verso la vista del fiume. Alcuni arredi fissi dello studio seguono il raggio di curvatura della parete espositiva, sottolineando così la soluzione d'insieme e unendo in un'unica forma compositiva lo studio conclusivo al percorso architettonico che parte dall'ingresso. Anche la camera da letto presistente è stata oggetto di un'attenta riqualificazione da cui emerge il mobile su disegno, di legno naturale con mensole di rame, che segna un'intera parete con il dinamico gioco volumetrico delle sue parti.

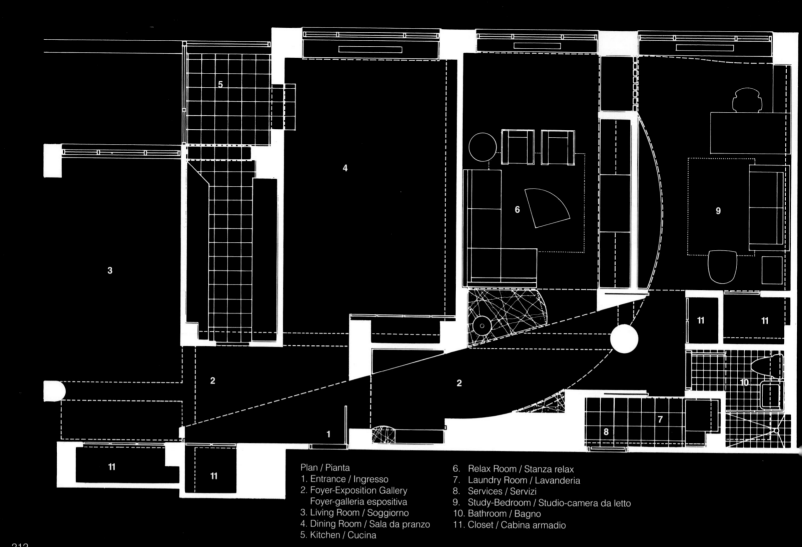

Plan / Pianta
1. Entrance / Ingresso
2. Foyer-Exposition Gallery
   Foyer-galleria espositiva
3. Living Room / Soggiorno
4. Dining Room / Sala da pranzo
5. Kitchen / Cucina

6. Relax Room / Stanza relax
7. Laundry Room / Lavanderia
8. Services / Servizi
9. Study-Bedroom / Studio-camera da letto
10. Bathroom / Bagno
11. Closet / Cabina armadio

212

Axonometric view / Assonometria

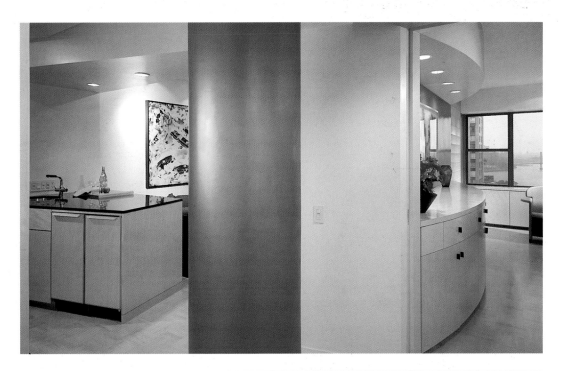

SCHEDE TECNICHE
TECHNICAL DATA

CHROMATIC RIGOR

Size
2.000 sq. ft.
Program
This loft in New York City's Flatiron District was designed as a showcase for art and entertaining.

The loft's owner is a public relations executive, with an extensive contemporary art collection, who frequently uses his residence for entertaining business clients.

A series of horizontal platforms and vertical planes expand and contract the space, organizing the Owner's project.

Bathrooms are at the core of the building; living, study and sleeping areas are at the perimeter, while the entry/gallery space serves as a connector.

Color is used to bridge architecture (fixed elements) with interior design (objects).

Three colors inspired by the paintings of Brice Marden determine the project's palette, and serve to define both the space and texture of the interior design.

The colors -- chocolate brown, blue/gray and black/blue -- first appear in (3) integral color plaster planes, which delineate the entry/gallery space and the living/study space at opposite ends of the loft. All other materials and textures derive from these three surfaces.

The floor serves as the palette's connecting element, where the warmth of oak is allowed to penetrate a blue/gray stain, fusing the three colors of the palette in one surface. The floor adjacent to the brown plaster wall appears blue, adjacent to the blue/gray wall it appears brown, etc. All other walls and ceilings are white and act as a neutral background for the artwork.

A series of gray, brown and blue variations of cloth and leather are used for the sofas and chairs. Custom designed tables utilize a dyed ash. Individual groupings of furniture are conceived to create three-dimensional paintings.

The art collection is dispersed in such a way as to encourage one's movement through the space. Asymmetrical placement leads the eye from one position to the next. The composition is designed to harmonize with the articulation of the spaces, while the lighting is designed to enhance this relationship.

Color, composition and lighting serve to integrate furnishings, space and art.

Rooms
gallery, living, dining, kitchen, study, master bedroom, master bath, guest bedroom, guest bath.
Materials
integral color plaster walls, stained oak wood floor, stainless steel (kitchen and bathrooms), custom millwork (study, kitchen, bedrooms)
Completed: May 1998
Project Team
Mark Janson, AIA, Hal Goldstein, AIA; partners in charge: Ceci Loebl, Project Manager
Lighting Designer: Craig Roberts Associates
Contractor: On the Level Enterprises, Inc.
Structural Engineer: Robert Silman & Associates
Mechanical Engineer: I.P.Group & Associates
Plaster: Art in Construction
Millwork Contractor: Bottino Designs
Furniture Fabricator: Decorative Arts Studio
Upholstered Furniture: Furniture Masters
Entrance
Artist: Brice Marden
Plaster by Art In Construction, New York,NY.
Artist: Wolfgang Laiab
Plaster by Art In Construction, New York,NY.
Living room
Brno Chairs by Knoll, Leather by Ashbury Hides, CA.
Plaster by Art In Construction, New York,NY.
Artist: Anish Kapoor
Table design by ARCHITECTUREPROJECT LLP.
Table fabricated by Decorative Arts Studio - Housatonic, Mass.
Artist: Art Guys.
Artist: Marina Ramuvick.
Plaster by Art In Construction, NY.
Artist: Anish Kapoor
Artist: Louis Sciullo
Tables designed ARCHITECTUREPROJECT LLP. Table
Fabricated by Decorative Arts Studio - Housatonic, Mass.
Brno Chairs by Knoll, Leather by Ashbury Hides.
Rug by Beauvais Carpet, New York, NY.
Side chair by Furniture Masters - Brooklyn, NY. Fabric by Rogers and Goffigon, LTD.
Bench Pads by Furniture Masters - Brooklyn, NY. Fabric by Rogers and Goffigon, LTD.
Shades: Mechoshade.

Artist: Vernon Fisher.
Owner's own furniture by Knoll. Designer: Mies van der Rohe, Barcelona Daybed and Table.
Artist: Tatsuo Miyajima.Plaster by Art In Construction, NY.
Finn Juhl Table, circa 1950's. Full House, New York, NY.
Artist: Vernon Fisher.
Owner's own furniture by Knoll. Designer Mies van der Rohe, Barcelona Daybed and Table. Bench Pads by Furniture Masters - Brooklyn, NY. Fabric by Rogers and Goffigon, LTD. Couch by Furniture Masters- Brooklyn, NY. Fabric by Rogers and Goffigon, LTD. Jean Michel Frank Table Lamps by Mattaliano. Holly Hunt New York.
Rug by Beauvais Carpet, New York, NY.
Artist: Yasumasa Morimura.
Studio
Artist: Richard Long.
Brno Chairs by Knoll, Leather by Ashbury Hides, CA.
Jean Michel Frank Chairs and Ottoman by Pucci International, New York, NY.
Plaster by Art In Construction, New York,NY.
Bedroom
Artist: Louis Sciullo.
Brno Chairs by Knoll, Leather by Ashbury Hides,CA.
Table design by ARCHITECTUREPROJECT LLP. Table
Fabricated by Decorative Arts Studio - Housatonic, Mass.
Artist: Sugimoto.
Artist: Micha Leksier.
Bathroom
Fixtures by Kroin.
American Olean Tile.
Artist: Duane Michaels.
Fixtures by Grohe.
Kitchen
Artist: Joel Peter Witkin.
Jacobsen Chairs. Troy, New York,NY.
Cabinetry by Bottino Design, Norwalk, CT.
Refrigerator and Dishwasher - Frigidaire Gallery.
Stove and Vent by Thermador.

TRIBECA LOFT

Size and Program
Project type: speculative real estate loft conversion of an existing building 40.000 sq. ft. loft conversion (condominium), 5 residential floors, 2 commercial floors 5.000 sq. ft. per floor. Total: 7 residential lofts, sizes: 1770 sq. ft. 2.350 sq. ft. and 3.500 sq. ft. penthouse duplex
Construction cost: $120/sq. ft. for interior construction of individual lofts
Design time: 3 months
Construction time: 18 months, completed 6/1997
Real Estate market: placed on the market in February 1997. All residential units were sold by February 1998, with prices from $590K to $1.4 mil. Total market value of the condominium was +/- 7 mil.

In the midst of a condominium market boom in New York City, this project, like many other similar 'real-estate ventures', was intended as an efficient conversion of an existing industrial building into residential lofts. It had to be designed as neutrally as possible, since the buyers' preferences were not known and it had to harmonize with Tribeca's current design trends. The design had to be "open" in response to the real estate criteria dictated by the market's demands. While remaining incomplete ("open"), to allow a specific buyer to finalize it on the basis of personal preferences and needs, the design had to be complete, to preserve its integrity. This complete incompleteness was a real challenge.

All the design decisions were based on marketing strategy: lofts had to be attractive to buyer(s) and developer. The design had to respond to two conflicting demands; to those of a prospective buyer, they had to look as high end as possible, while they had to be as inexpensive to build as possible for the developer. While construction costs for custom lofts in New York may run as high as $300/sq. ft., the real-estate industry is willing to spend approximately $100/sq. ft. The building fully covers (100 %) a typical downtown Manhattan lot. It is a block-through building with a lot size equal to 25' x 200'. It faces Duane Street on the South and Thomas Street on the North. The typical floor plate is therefore "long and narrow. Toward the middle of the floor plate there is almost no natural light. The building has large windows only on street fronts and one small lot line window at the back part of each loft.

The idea was to design lofts where living areas are implied and not fixed and lofts feel as open as possible. The open quality of the space had to be receptive to many possible uses and interpretations. They are composed of flowing, interconnected "modern" spaces, not rooms; however, all the amenities required by real estate industry standards (two bathrooms, or a bathroom and a powder room, walk-in closet, laundry/utility room and a kitchen, in addition to living/dining area, den /study and sleeping area) had to be included. To resolve this paradox, the design clustered all the requirements of 'secondary spaces' (bath-

216

rooms, walk-in closet, utility room, and kitchen) together in the utility core, creating a "floating" cluster in the long and narrow box-like container of the loft's 'primary space'. The "floating" effect has necessitated a lack of full-height walls, with the exception of core walls, which encase tubing servicing the entire building. The key challenge was to find the right proportion and scale of spaces and their allocation, maintaining the nature of the open loft space, to "fill-in" the space without "filling" it in. The "filling" core was obtained by creating an interplay between loosely connected spaces. This has permitted a continuity of space by eliminating a single focal compositional element. Instead of being distinctly separate, the areas of the loft are linked by a visual effect that was provided by placing the compositional core between the two corridors; thereby maintaining the open-space characteristic. We liked to call this design strategy 'Swiss cheese' (multiple holes within one body).

The lack of windows in the 'middle' section of the loft was supplemented by multiple vistas and viewing corridors revealing the loft's distinct rooms. As a result, each loft opens onto itself. Views to the exterior were replaced with interior views of the loft. Glass enclosures (boxes) over the bathrooms are just one example of these openings. They were conceived as "interior windows". At night, when these boxes are internally lit and the rest of the loft is in dimmed darkness, one may get a very small-scale effect of the 'New York skyline' with 'rooms in the air'.

Bathrooms have white Grecian marble floors and walls, stainless steel sinks and maple vanity cabinets. Kitchens have honed Bronzino stone counter tops, maple kitchen cabinets and top quality stainless steel kitchen appliances. Each loft has a private elevator access, individual central heating and air conditioning, and phone and cable TV wiring at every 25' throughout the loft.

EXPOSED STRUCTURE

Project: Silvia Dainese with Sergio Corazza
Year: 1993/94
Floor Area: 2000 sq. Ft.
Address: 39 Northmoore Street, New York.

Floors:
Wood floors: Brazilian Cherry gibs
Master bathroom: floor, bathtub, sink and shelves in unpolished, sand-colored, limestone slabs, deigned by Manhattan Marble Co. (267 Elizabeth street, New York).

Ceilings:
Restored and sanded original beams; exposed in the day area and used with gypsum panels resting on the I-beam to create a suspended ceiling in the night zone and the bathroom.
Electric and air conditioning system placed in the suspended ceiling.

Furniture:
Custom-made wall closets in maple between the bathroom and the master bedroom, designed by Mascot Interiors (198 North 4th street, Brooklyn).
Kitchen cabinets in maple, designed by Mascot Interiors; base, backsplash and shelves in white Carrara marble from Marble Co.; stainless steel cabinet doors in pulled netting by Coges (1, Via Belgio, Padova, Italy). Custom-made carpentry work by John DeLorenzo & Bro., Inc. (45 Grand Street, New York). Taps by Arne Jacobsen and created by KROIN for the kitchen. In the master bathroom, taps by Czech & Speake, sink shelves in iron with exposed joints in plate and brass (Manhattan Marble Co.). Semi-circular bookshelves in mdf and aluminium and mdf sandwich rods, made by Contin, Ltd. (4 Via IV Novembre, Thiene, Vicenza, Italy).
Lighting by Santa & Cole, supplied by Eleber Illuminotecnica (50, Corso San Felice, Vicenza, Italy).
Kleis doorknobs by RDS for maple the wood doors, while the handles for the running doors were made on a design by Di più (8, Selciato San Nicolò, Padova).

Walls:
For the night area, the walls were treated with an ochre plaster finish on gypsum, created by Yon Verwer (228 West Broadway, 6th floor, New York); the north and east walls are in original exposed brick, which has been sanded and painted white, while the west wall has been covered in gypsum panels and white tempera.

Artwork:
The running door that separates the open space from the night area is an original piece by a street artist.

Doors/Windows:
Maple wood doors for the private rooms and running wall doors with an ochre plaster finish in the bathroom, created by Mascot Interiors.

FIXED SCENE

Size
5.000 sq.ft. loft on the fifth floor of a converted warehouse, for an art collector.

Residuary Continuities
"It is not the conduct of bodies but, rather, the conduct of something that existed between them, i.e. the field, that could be essential for ordering and interpreting all events."
Albert Einstein

For the Wooster Street project, we were asked to adapt the 5th floor of a converted SOHO loft building to residential space for an art collector. This highly urban living condition reflects the "nomadic" quality of today's metropolis. As the owner travels between London and New York, internet was the primary mode of communication during the project.

'LOFT = existing space', manipulated. Reconstituted, with additions and divisions. Standard residential elements reformulated to create spatial continuities.

In designing the loft, various living spaces were created, such as public/private areas or guest rooms, and the concept of "connective cuts" was developed. Translucent panels serve as connective components, which, when cut (or sliced) become suspended, pivotal compositional elements.

A 'kitchen' is spaced within the 'fold' of a wall section, its work surfaces suspended. As the sectional plane is sliced, several areas can be projected simultaneously. The aluminum cabinets form a thin sliver band, while recessed lights illuminate the work surfaces below. Two cantilevered surfaces flank the kitchen and a fixed cement-finish work surface hovers over a pivoting breakfast bar, made of poured polyurethane.

Created to function as a 'separate' entity, the fireplace is situated away from the wall, designed as a transparent hearth. Acting as a screen from which one can see to the other side, the fire from this hearth warms the room, altering the ambience.

A free-floating bathroom has been designed as a capsule, its separate functions unified in a glass pane 'wrapping', which physically divides the spaces. The steam of the hot water that frosts the panes is evidence of the capsule's true function.

As a result, areas or 'fields of occupation' have been formed, a continuous flowing space running between them. Texture changes in the walls, floors and windows further designate these areas as hard, soft and neutral spaces. Doors and enclosures are replaced by shifts in volume, and transitions into different areas become "hinge-points", while providing visual privacy. Overall, the continuity of these interlocking volumes creates a residence of overlapping intersections and interweaving space.

Floor
Ardex floor: custom color, self leveling seamless poured floor by Pyramid Floor Covering, with recessed sisal carpet (Clodan)

Bedrooms & Library
wide plank hardwood floor in white oak, Walnut custom designed library shelves and desk.

Furniture
Troy NY- Moss NY- Sofa's: B&B Italia-Eames dining chairs: Modern Age NY
Guest-bed frames: ROTO Architects, LA Techno Nomos table frame with custom gray glass table top; walk-in closets, custom-made furniture (master bed, low table on wheels, pivot tables, etc.): Poliform;

Walls
Art in Construction plaster, concrete wash walls
Custom stainless steel & glass wall by United Aluminum, NY with Sumi glass

Ceiling
a folded gypsum integral ceiling

Master Bathroom
Art in Construction waterproof structural plaster; fixtures in stainless steel, Metcraft ss. suspended toilets; Kroin faucets; mirror from Modern Stone Age, NY Walnut custom designed wall with hidden cabinets, custom designed bed in walnut veneer and antracite plaster. Custom designed free-standing fireplace finished in antracite plaster with Rais&Wittus fireplace inset.

Guest Bathroom
Orange Glass Nemo tiles and Art in Construction Plaster; stainless sink from Wall Lights: Drop 2 from Flos, Italy (Moss)

Small Bathroom
stainless steel walls & ceiling; Metcraft stainless steel toilet; Kroin faucets. Wardrobe: Walnut veneer custom designed.

Library: Master bedroom
Glass block lights: MOMA store NY. Standing light: Troy NY.

Curtains
Ultra suede of Toray America and steel mesh curtains from: Cascade Coil Drapery. Wall light: "Warrior" of Artemide

Kitchen area
Boffi stainless steel suspended kitchen cabinets and glass and aluminum top cabinets with integral lighting. Miele cooktop, oven and dishwasher, and SubZero refrigerator. Milkbottle light by Tejo Remy (Moss, NY)

Project team
Architect: Archi-Tectonics, NYC, Architect: Winka Dubbeldam
Team: Roemer Pierik, Joachim Karelse, Bernd Kornberger
Contractor: A.J. Greenwich Contracting
Cabinetry: Black Oak Design Services.
Structural Engineer: Yury Marinyansky of Severud Associates
Mechanical Engineer: Stan Slutsky Engineers
Fabric fabrications: Milena Jevremov.

Stereo installation: Stereo Exchange Inc., NY

DOMESTIC SCENES

Size
1.400 sq.ft. loft renovation for achoreographer.
Site/Context
It is located on the ninth floor of an industrial loft building on lower Fifth Avenue. The space is north facing with minimal natural light.
Proposal/Strategies
Using transparent, translucent and opaque materials, the project establishes several types of interchangeable programmatic relationships and connections within a tight space.

The space is organized through a series of dynamic planes running longitudinally from the entry to the window wall. These planes range from glass rods and various types of plate glass to sliding fin-ply and glass panels which mediate the relationship of the program and space on either side. For instance, the guest room is adjacent to the kitchen and can become a dining area by opening the sliding panels or can become privately linked to the bathroom by closing the panels. The materials of these primary organizing planes are used in other locations to establish associations between traditionally separated domestic programs. These associations are further developed through slate, cork and cherry flooring which extend under the planes to connect adjacent spaces.
Design Citation, American Institute of Architects, New York Chapter; 1997
Rooms
Two bedrooms (one flexible to be used as office and/or guest bedroom) and two bathrooms, open kitchen with dining and living space
1400 s.f. located on Fifth Avenue at 18th Street
Floor:
Entry and guest bath - slate/ Kitchen and guest bedroom/office - cork/Living/Dining and bedroom - cherry wood/Bathroom - glass tile
Ceiling
gypsum board
Walls
gypsum board, slate in guest bath, glass and acrylic rods at bedrooms, glass tile at bathroom
Cabinets
stainless steel in kitchen and bath, cherry in dining
Furniture
daybed, bed, airmoire, bedside table, entry table special shelves by Chris Lerecke
Lighting
Wall sconces by David Weeks
Miscellaneous
candle holders and miscellaneous elements by Ted Muehling
Sliding Panels: Fin-Ply, glass.

SELF-CONSTRUCTION

Size
2.000 sq.ft
Program
The building is brick perimeter structure with wood columns, beams and joists making up the interior structure of the building. The loft was a watch band factory prior to renovation and pieces of watch bands such as the buckles have made permanent imprints in the floor. The loft was under renovation for 2 1/2 years and was built by Beth and Paul with some assistance from friends. Living in the loft during the course of the renovation influenced the detailing and programming of the design. The project had three phases based on the column divisions. The kitchen and bath fell outside of this phasing: the kitchen was "sketched" and made temporarily functional until the final phase and the bathroom was completed early in the project. The film "Afraid of Everything", directed by David Barker and released in 1999, was filmed in the loft in December 1997 prior to the loft's completion.

The goal of the design was to define spaces along a semi- traditional breakdown (e.g. kitchen, library, etc.) while building as few rooms as possible. This was achieved through the placement of wall planes, built in furnishings and definition of programmed zones. Apart from closets, the only rooms completely defined by walls are the bedroom and the bathroom and the laundry. The three skylights, at the library, kitchen and entry sink, serve to further define these spaces while introducing light to the inner areas of the loft.

The exposed sprinkler, electrical and plumbing piping create a diagram of systems whose background is the ceiling.

The windowsills are cast-in-place concrete and extend 9" from the window providing a ledge for plants and cats while also making a window threshold.

Black pipe and Hollaender "Speed-rail" fittings were used as a structural baseline in the project from the support of the tub and counter tops in the kitchen to the bookcases, tables and bed.

Floor:
maple with water-based polyurethane
Ceiling
plaster
Furniture
all chairs except Eames chair and Stickley rocker are refurbished off-the-street finds. The table was constructed of 2 x 6 Douglas fir, black pipe, Speed-rail fittings and Component Hardware adjustable feet and casters.
Walls: exterior walls are painted brick, interior walls are plaster and gypsum wall board
Doors
all doors are refurbished off-the-street finds.
Plumbing Fixtures
all fixtures are re-furbished off-the-street finds.
Artworks
"Forest Fire" pastel by Joe Goode, Untitled oil painting by James Reinke, Untitled photograph by Paul Warchol, "Brooklyn Bridge Analysis Model" by Beth Sigler, "Blue Pitcher" by Anna Blackwell, "Casa Malaparte Analysis Model" by Paul Henderson.

URBAN ATELIER

Furniture and Artworks
Living Level
Aluminum and glass table by A. Skurman.
Paintings by Joan Waltemath, Babette Allina, Taro Suzuki
Construction: Pierre Louaver
Drapes: Monte Coleman
Bertoia Chair: Knoll
Light: Lightolier
Studio
Eileen Gray's tubular steel table with white laminate top is flanked by galvanized steel cafe chairs.

LIVEABLE READY-MADE

Program
Located in the garment district in Midtown Manhattan, the Miller-Jones Studio results from the conversion of a commercial loft into the residence/work space for a fashion photographer and a set designer. The loft, on the 14th floor, enjoys southern exposure and exciting Manhattan cityscapes through a 30, long window. After returning it to its industrial definition (high ceiling, concrete floor and white walls), a bidimensional element (the side of a 40' long aluminum shipping container) is inserted to define a shear edge between private and professional needs.

The container wall cuts across the warehouse space and intersects different functions along its axis. Only technological appliances emerge when it is completely closed. A system of incisions breaks it into a mechanism of rotating panels that, when opened, re-establish the continuity of the spaces revealed behind them: bedroom, kitchen, and storage.

The side of the container penetrates the bathroom to become the shower partition.

Floating in the main space, an island on casters, made out of 4 refrigerators lying on their sides, encapsulates all work functions. The refrigerators serve as storage while their doors serve as additional work surfaces when lifted open. A wood top on tracks is parted down the middle and pulls out to create two desks at opposite ends of the island. One end is equipped with a drafting board that slides on its own tracks, while the computer is imbedded in the refrigerator body at the other end. The scanner and printer slide out of the former freezer compartment. Both ends are furnished with a pullout lamp and electric outlets.

Description
The structure of the loft is a cement structure. The floor is left exposed throughout the apartment, while walls and ceilings are painted white.
The inside structure that holds the aluminum container siding is a wood structure (wood studs, 4x8 inch section), compressed between floor and ceiling, and finished with black rubber coating.
Living room/studio
Marshmallow sofa by George Nelson; Warren McCarthur chairs; Charcoal drawings by Cristine Jones (back wall).
Bedroom
Charles Eames airport seating; George Nelson clocks (on top of file cabinets).

ORIENTAL FLAVORS

Size
The 2.300 sq.ft loft designed by G.Phillip Smith and Douglas Thompson is on the top floor of a former clothing manufacturing building off Gramercy Park.

218

Program

The space had previously been renovated for residential use; however, the new owners required a completely new arrangement. Newly married, the two executives had lived in Japan and wanted an efficiently detailed environment, suggestive of Japanese simplicity with abundant, accessible storage.

Of particular interest was the development of a study/guest room on the roof above and an inviting access to the potentially large roof terrace, to which they have exclusive rights.

Layouts of the rooms from the former renovation were, for the most, part, maintained. Sliding doors offered the best solution for providing handicapped access, as required by the regulations.

A glass staircase has maintained the view from the entrance onto the north-facing windows, which overlook the Empire State and Chrysler buildings. The living/dining area has been placed along this windowed wall, preserving the dramatic view, which extends along the 48 foot length of the apartment. The kitchen alcove also opens onto this space.

Bedrooms and bathrooms are concealed by a vestibule created by an angled wall and the staircase that leads to the upper level. A false ceiling was built into this area to create overhead storage compartments similar to those used in airplanes. The ribbon like profile of the staircase is structured by a series of tansuchests and cabinets that have been painted in subtle hues to highlight their different uses. They require no handles because each "drawer" is set on a different plane. Thereby creating handles through the resulting spaces.

Maple wood was used throughout. In the kitchen a poured black resin countertop, like those used in laboratories harmonizes with the acid washed steel used in other areas of the loft. Also in the kitchen, a portion of the original brick wall was retained to maintain the original workspace.

Mobile storage compartments in the entertainment area, by the fireplace, contain audio equipment and may be rearranged according to the desired seating arrangement. Dressing chairs in the master bath open for storage and allow space to be used in a flexible manner.

On the upper level an enclosure was devised at the top of the stairs to provide a buffer against noise. A large window in the enclosure lights the staircase and the interior of the loft, below.

Materials
Oak strip flooring
Resin countertops
Sandblasted and painted glass
Maple staircase with acid washed, 20 ft. one-piece steel tailing
Entrance and living room artwork by Richard Kreshtool

THE VALUE OF SPACE

Floors
Living Area, Dining Area and Kitchen: Serena stone, 60cm x 60cm
Bedroom: Red Oak. Master bathroom: pine green marble, white Carrara trim and details of floor and walls
Guest Bathroom: white ceramic tile with blue trim, floors and walls
Ceilings and walls: white plaster throughout
Kichen: white glass with decorative trim
Living / Dining area, kitchen and Study/Office: white plaster
Master Bedroom: Red Oak paneling
Windows: anodized black aluminum with insulated glass and thermal "tilt and turn" handles
Furniture and furnishings:
Living Room: Arflex Strips
Lighting and floor lamps: Ingo Maurer
Low table: custom design by Studio MORSA (Antonio Morello)
Upholstered Armchairs: suede, custom design by Studio MORSA (Antonio Morello)
Rolling Library Shelving, Kitchen, and all Storage Areas: custom design by Studio MORSA in Red Oak with white pigmented finish
Study/Office sofa: Flexform; desk: Zanotta
Master bedroom: custom design by Studio MORSA in Red Oak with a natural finish
Artwork:
Paintings by Luis Oliver
Sculpture byAntonio Morello

OPEN SPACE

Floor:
Living areas: Brazilian Cherry
Kitchen/Entry Foyer/Laundry/Guest Bath: Farges limestone
Master Bath: Ancient Marble
Ceiling:
Living areas: painted wood joists/steel beams.
Other areas: dining table by Carlos Scarpa; dining chairs by GF

Fireproof aluminum office furniture (circa 1948)
Dining Room:
Chandelier by Arne Jacobsen, 1949
Living Room sofa by Jean Michel Frank; coffee table by Wyeth, NY; carpet by Picasso,1934; red armchair: 30 Bond St.; Sideboard by Paul Frankl,1928
Master Bath:
Lithograph by John Shaw
Walls: painted sheetrock
Windows
Mahogany
Doors: Quarter-sawn ash

SPACES IN LINE

Floor
Living areas/Entry gallery/Study: American Cherry
Kitchen: tapestry, granite tile
Ceilings:
Master Bath: tumbled wood joists/steel beams
Other areas: painted gypsum board
Furniture:
Living Areas: dining table and chairs by Frank Lloyd Wright,
Mirror: Amandanali, NY
Walls: painted gypsum board
Windows: aluminum
Doors: Beech wood doors, painted frames, cherry and frosted glass

Apartments

ABSOLUTE SPACES

Size
The 3.000 sq. ft. apartment occupies a dramatic site on Park Avenue (Manhatten). It has with 4 windows and three terraces with a total surface area of 1.000 sq. ft.
Program
The design solution's low ceiling and continuous 1m. by 1m. Arria limestone floor create an abstract spatial field. The programmed spaces were defined by the wall and the discrete free-standing areas. The apartment's central areas, the living room, the study and the master bedroom, became like courtyards, emphasized by rooms of ribbon mahogany (containing closets to hide structures and risers) and illuminated by the glow of the bathroom, encased in glass.

Acting as a backdrop to a Modernist, 20th century photography collection, the palette echoes the tones of a monochromatic print. The walls and ceiling that define the perimeter are in white plaster while the bathroom plumbing, walls and fixtures are carved from blocks of white Sivec marble. Separating each bathroom from adjacent rooms are full-height opaque glass walls. In the master bath, the glass walls and sliding door are made from low-voltage privacy glass that can be switched to clear from the bath or bed, merging the two rooms. The floating spaces that define the main rooms are sheathed in mahogany, while the doors that divide these spaces are in satin-finished, stainless steel.

ASYMMETRIC MANIPULATIONS

Size
2.300 sq. ft.
Program
This project represents the transformation of a traditional Manhattan apartment into a spatially complex modern loft. Asymmetrical formations create modern and dynamic spatial tensions that interact with the original structure.

Three exposed, original round-shaped columns support the original beams of the ceiling, emphasizing them and functioning as a "parasol" over the new plan and section.

The grid of the limestone floor is rotated from the existing orthogonal plan. Cabinet and bathroom walls are also rotated to reflect this shift.

The cabinets that enclose the study and the dressing rooms are "suspended" between the ceiling below and the glass panels above, ensuring privacy while maintaining an appearance of openness.

The undulating fireplace wall is "carved away," revealing the depth of the wall behind it. This sense of weight and density juxtaposes the openness of the plan. The fireplace is both traditional--a central feature in the apartment--and modern, in its manipulation away from the wall surface.

Designed for a married couple with grown children, the apartment comprises a living room, a formal dining area, an eat-in kitchen, a study, a library, a master bedroom suite with two dressing rooms, two bathrooms and a laundry room.

Materials are neutral and act as a backdrop for spatial interplay. They include limestone; maple and carpeted floors with painted wood baseboards; integrally colored veneer plaster and back-painted glass walls; perforated stainless steel stack enclosures; and wood and stainless steel cabinets with granite, limestone and onyx tops.

LIGHT AND COLOR

Size
790 sq. ft.
Program
The apartment is situated in Midtown Manhattan, just north of the U.N. Building. The building was constructed in 1929 for the purpose of renting affordable apartments to women commencing their careers in N.Y. Ironically, the client, an Australian, came to NY in 1996 as a publisher for a major American book publishing company.

The original layout had not taken advantage of its southern exposure and was limited by its various rooms and corridors, compacted into a small area.

The client had her furniture and artwork shipped from Australia, so that it could be incorporated into the project's design. Several new furniture pieces were acquired during the course of the project.

The client also requested bookshelves, though she did not want them to visually dominate the interior. Other requirements were a workable kitchen and adequate storage and dressing room area.

Floor - new floor
Oak, clear stained.
Ceiling
existing plaster on concrete slab.
Walls
painted plaster; and veneer panels - walnut and maple
Inside structure
existing steel column and beam structure encased in concrete.
Windows
existing painted timber frame.
Doors
hinged Maple/Walnut integral with wall panel system.- sliding doors, walnut.
Bedhead
maple
Cabinetry/Bookshelves
white matt lacquer
Kitchen counter stainless steel
white glass splash backs.
Handles and knobs
D Line stainless steel.
Fireplace
existing carrara.

Furniture
Living room
Mies van der Rohe chaise *, Pierre Chareau sofa, Mies van der Rohe coffee table *, Gordon Mather ottoman, Arne Jacobson chairs, George Nelson bench *, Carlo Forcollini standard lamps
* new acquisitons
Dining
Le Corbusier LC6 table and LC8chairs
Bedroom
G. Rietveld table, Tolemeo desk lamp
New ceiling lights
' Ra ' fittings designed by King and Miranda
Artworks (Living room)
Dali print "LINCOLN in DALIVISION"-MARALINGA painting by Jonathon Kumuntjara Brown - Susan Norrie painting (above fireplace) - Corrugated rusted steel map of Australia by Geoff Jones

ARCHITECTURAL SURFACES

Size
2.000 sq. ft.
Program
The client purchased this 1946 Emery Roth apartment for the location and the views. After several programming meetings Gerner Kronick + Valcarcel suggested that in order to fulfil the client's needs, the apartment should be entirely gutted. Proceeding on that premise, a modern, open area apartment was created, using a minimalist palette.

Completed in 1946, the apartment is 2,000 sq. ft. Since its construction, the owner, who had lived there the entire time, had never carried out any work on the structure. Needless to say, it was in bad shape. The client required a New York City apartment primarily for entertainment purposes, but also as a place to sleep occasionally and as a place in which their sons could stay during their visits to the city. GKV decided to demolish the existing areas and create a large unified

space, emphasizing the view on Central Park. Three storage areas were added, made from custom millwork and finished in three subtle shades of colored lacquer. The east-west axis of the apartment was defined by custom millwork panels in French Walnut, which house large storage cabinets. One living room walls is composed of a full-height set of panels in unfilled travertine. An intricate and adjustable lighting system was inserted into the ceiling, which was lowered by 2". A state of the art AV system and a centralized air conditioning system have also been installed.

Floor
American White Oak, bleached and pickled; custom carpets.
Ceiling
Painted gypsum wall board.
Walls
Travertine- French Walnut - Colored Lacquer -Painted gypsum wallboard
Furniture
Custom upholstered pieces by De Angelis - custom tables by Walter P. Sauer - custom rugs by Edward Fields - custom windows
Structure
Original steel structure encased in concrete
Windows
original
Bathrooms
Mahogany wall panels with marble mosaic floor; two other bathrooms with marble floors and walls.
Kitchen
Lacquer cabinets with granite counter tops and backsplash.
Furniture
Living Room
Custom tables designed by GKV and made by Walter P. Sauer; custom upholstered pieces by De Angelis; custom carpet by Edward Fields; fabrics by J. Robert Scott.
Dining Room
Cutom table designed by GKV and made by Walter P. Sauer; custom travertine pedestal by Domestic Stone and Marble; console table designed by GKV and made by Domestic Stone and Marble.
Light fixtures by Louis Poulsen.
Library
Upholstered pieces by Avery Boardman.
Chair by B & B Italia.
Desk custom designed by GKV and made by Nordic Interiors Woodwork.
Lamp by Louis Poulsen.
Carpet by Edward Fields.
Fabrics by J. Robert Scott.
Master Bedroom
Bed by Avery Boardman.
Custom nightstands by Nordic Interiors Woodwork.
Custom benches by De Angelis.
Lamps by Artemede.
Fabrics by J. Robert Scott.
Carpet by Edward Fields.
Guest Bedroom
Bed by Avery Boardman.
Millwork by Nordic Interiors Woodwork.
Chest by B & B Italia.
Fabrics by J. Robert Scott.
Carpet by Edward Fields.
Kitchen
Custom millwork by Nordic Interiors Woodwork.
Granite countertops and backsplash by Domestic Stone and Marble.
Floors: American White Oak, bleached and pickled.
Bathroom
Floors: custom marble mosaics by Domestic Stone and Marble.
Mahogany wall panels by Nordic Interiors Woodwork.

DRESSED SPACES

Living Room
Custom maple floors: lothar cords; paint for walls and ceilings: Benjamin Moore; custom chaise, sofa, lounge chairs, upholstered wall fabrics by K.Flam Associates; chaise fabric by Clarence House; chenille throw by Myung Jin; lounge chairs and sofa fabric by Manuel Canovas; ottoman by George Smith; upholstered wall fabric by Design Tex; grass boxes and orchids by Floribellium; silver tray by Bergdorf Goodman; photo on floor by Berenice Abbott New York; large mirror by Betty Jane Bart; custom console by Edward R.Butler Co.; deco lamp by David Duncan.
Dining Room
is awash in light. Fashion inspirations include sheer tutus on the chairs. Biedermeier table and chairs by Legendary Collections; slipcover fabric for Biedermeier chairs by Jack Lenor Larsen; dining chair seat fabric by J. Robert Scott;

slipcover fabric by Design Tex

Home Office (it also doubles as a guest bedroom)

Carpet by Rosecore; windows, bench and pillow fabrics by K. Flam Associates; window fabric by Lee Jofa/Groundworks; window bench fabric by Manuel Canovas; sleep sofa by Avery Boardman; sleep sofa fabric by Decorator's Walk; pillow fabric by Donghia; Robsjohn-Gibbings desk by Full house; center table by See; metal lamp by David Landis Design; wall lamp by Through Lees Studio.

Bathroom

The shower is an engineering miracle, its large glass panel supported by only by two hinges. Shower door by Architectural Glass Craft; custom bath accessories by BNO Collection through Edward R. Butler; antique mirror restoration by EliC. Rios.

The Master Bedroom

has a spectacular view, which incorporates the interiors' thematic elements.
Carpet by Rosecore; window, bedspread and headboard by K. Flam Associates; window by Lee Jofa/Groundworks; chaise by Donghia; chaise fabric by Kirk Brummel; throw by Jeffery Aronoff; bedspread by Clarence House; linens by Chambers; tablecloth and boxspring leather by Cortina Leather; wall lamp by Nessen Lighting; artwork by Aero Studio.

THE COLLECTOR'S HOME

Entrance vestibule

Floors: flamed steel panels with stainless steel inserts
Ceiling: perforated aluminum
Furnishings: painted steel beam and rods, glass shelf

Central Gallery

Floors: flamed steel panels and sisal rug
Furnishings: custom sandblasted steel and glass pedestal, Cor-ten steel pedestal

Conversation Room

Floors: flamed steel panels, polished granite and sisal rug
Ceiling: fiberglass vault with custom aluminum grills for HVAC, lighting and music distribution.
Walls: two-layered motorized drapes for views and natural lighting control
Windows: inner sliding glass frame for noise reduction
Furnishings: custom sandblasted steel daybeds with fabric and leather cushions, lacquered tables, Cor-ten steel pedestal

Studio

Floors: flamed steel panels, sisal rug
Walls: motorized PVC blinds
Furnishings: custom polyester-resin modular units, aluminum leaf finish table

Library

Floors: flamed steel panels with neoprene strips, raised tempered glass floor plane on steel pegs.
Walls: electrified, separable aluminum panels with custom-pattern. Each panel is fed by a low voltage system for lighting. Steel desk with concrete counterweights; motorized hospital bed; sliding daybed on curved aluminum track mounted to floor; custom lighting; bookcase with polyester-resin finish, glass shelving.

Structural Engineer: Szayer Engineers
Mechanical/electrical: Mosher and Doran
Lighting: Lightron of Cornwall
Glass Platforms: Amses Cosma
Contractor: Quinn Construction Group

DETAIL AND IRONY

Size

850 sq.ft.

Program

"Mod is in the Details"
Has wry New York designer Marco Pasanella stopped laughing? In the subdued renovation of his Manhattan residence, the witty designer, best known for his sideways rocking chair, seems to have quieted his tone
Of course not, Pasanella replies,."I've just learned to cover my mouth. With park views and high ceilings," the designer explains, "the challenge was not to create a great space. It was already pretty great. The hard part was to try to keep me excited about coming home day after day. How does one keep a sense of discovery of inventiveness of joy? Often a wink makes me happier than a slap on the back. After a 12 hour day in the studio, the last thing I want to see when I get home is D-E-S-I-G-N. The key, I realized, was to think small, smart and fun".

The one-bedroom apartment deserves a detailed observation. Looking around the sober sage-colored living room, for instance, one discovers that the limestone mantelpiece features Pasanella's version of a big game trophy, a stuffed goldfish. "Teddy Roosevelt-turned-upside-down," Marco observes.

Likewise, scanning the family portraits, one comes upon a silver gilt frame that states 'Space Available'. The bathroom appears to be a gentlemanly and distinct room until one stumbles upon a smiling picture of the designer mounted on the toilet seat. Then, what look like cologne bottles are, in fact, Santeria botanicals with names like Woman Magnet and Chains Breaker. Similarly, the kitchen features a rack which displays hanging cookware and pictures of loved ones.

This apartment, however, is packed with more than just a series of design winks. As Pasanella explains, "a lot of the things that make you smile, also make a lot of sense. Like the [bedroom] curtain with the hole in it, which frames a view out, but doesn't let passing bus drivers see in. The designer has also incorporated his much-lauded line of double function furniture, which he admits, "I really designed with myself in mind." His reading settee, for example, saves storage space as it a combination lounge chair and bookshelf. In the kitchen, one of Pasanella's Soup's On Tables with inlaid place settings is paired with stowaway chairs in the kitchen, which provide perches for extra sections of the notoriously space-hogging New York Times.

Putting his spin on an ancient saying, Pasanella smiles, "my home is a place where mod is in the details".

EXPOSITIONAL ELEGANCE

Size

3.100 sq.ft.

Program

In this Fifth Avenue apartment, strong architecture harmonizes with bold modern art and African sculpture, without overpowering the sense of a home or turning the art into decoration. Large wood wall panels, pedestals, niches and juxtaposed horizontal and vertical planes provide specific environments for the artwork. Rich furnishings and materials, like the planar marble mantle and the polished African mahogany floors, provide an artistic contrast to the objects, as do the angled, cushioned window seats framed by the lightly draped sheer fabric panels that act as curtains. Throughout the apartment, white, off-white and yellowish wood and dark gray tones blend with the furnishings. In the kitchen steel panels harmonize with fine wood paneling, marble backplashes and a handsome patterned wood floor. A thin border runs along the edge of the panels, ordering the dimensional ratio between the works of art and the spacious floor plan. A wonderful view of Central Park has been reserved for the bedroom.

Project Team

Henry Stolzman, Wayne Berg, Lea H. Cloud, Jonathan Schecter, Albert Ho, Elyse Hommel-Cohen, John Kelleher, Betty Liu, Emily Moss, Janet Roseff, Tim Witzg.
Interior Consultant: Tse-Yun Chu Studio, New York, New York
Lighting Consultant: Johnson Schwinghammer, New York, New York
Contractor: R.C.Dolner

LIVING WITH ART

Size

Size
1.800 sq. ft.

Major Interior Materials

Oak with ebony (floors), zinc (room entry; cantilevered living room display shelves), limestone (living room wall slabs), glass (dining room and living room wall panels), marble (terrace floor), sandblasted steel (terrace doors), frosted glass (bedroom and dining rooms pocket doors)

Furnishings and Storage

Custom designed by architect (terrace doors, bedroom vanity/night table, aluminum framed bed, study and dining room pocket doors, living room display shelves, built-in cabinetry),Ward Bennet (terrace chair),Ben Tre (terrace table), Gabriele Mucchi reproduction (bedroom chair), Mario Botta (black living room and some tables and chairs), Philippe Starck (dining room "Babarian Chair" in bronze and cowhide),Many of the items are from the owner's craft collection.

Artwork (from the owner's collection)

Lucie Suzuki, Soldner Rie, Peter Gilhoodi, Paula Voulkos, Robert Winokur, Christie Devoke Brown(ceramic pieces), Doug Fuchs, Claire Zeisler, Donna Look, Susan Lyman(fiber pieces), Joel Philip Myers, Colon Reid, Marion Uddesky (glass pieces),Wendy Richman Ramshaw (metal objects), Ed Moulthorp (wood piece).

Fixtures

P.E Guerin
Response to site and exiting structure:
This small apartment is located in a beaux-arts building on Fifth Avenue. Any period character that the interior may have had was eliminated in a 1950's "modernization" project, but a spectacular view of Central Park has remained. The design team's response was to expand the small, narrow interior with an open, fluid plan, while maintaining some sense of traditional room divisions. Another objective was to take advantage of the park view.

Design

The design process involved establishing a clear, consistent language of form and material, distilling essential design elements from unnecessary details. It was critical that the interior architecture act as a setting for the entry vestibule. Toward the front, the airy living room extends toward a glass-enclosed terrace, which acts as an "urban porch". Both the terrace and the bedroom adjacent to it are raised several inches, setting them apart from the rest of the interior. The terrace's steel-framed glass doors reveal Central Park and the skyline, while the collection pieces can be seen through them.

Construction

Materials chosen for their richness, warmth and solidity are: plated zinc, sand-blasted steel, ebony, oak and marble.

Project team

Henry Stolzman, Wayne Berg, FAIA; Lea H.Cloud, AIA; Nancy Cooper; Harley Swedler; Tse-Yun Chu
Consultants: Tse-Yun Chu Studio (materials and finishes), Jerry Kugler Associates (lighting design)
Engineers: Jack Green Associates (mechanical and electrical systems)
General Contractor: Embassy Construction

CENTRAL PARK WEST

Size

7.500 sq.ft.

Program

The challenge of creating a sophisticated modern residence in a grand old apartment building overlooking Central Park infuses this design by Lee Harris Pomeroy / Architects. The new residence combines two former L-shaped apartments into a unified space. The most arresting result of the newly integrated space is its view of Central Park, which spans the entire front of the building. This expansive vista provides the starting point and the focal point for the architectural design.

To take full advantage of the Central Park exposure, the architects tore out interior walls to create a long, linear, gallery-like space that extends 75 feet along the front of the building. All the primary living functions - reception, relaxation, dining, entertaining and service - coexist within this space. Since every window offers a dramatic view, the space was allowed to remain as open as possible. Divisions between the spaces are subtle, and often flexible, so that particular areas can be closed off by a system of pivoting walls and sliding partitions of fine-crafted mahogany.

An interior entrance hall is created by a partition consisting of a low mahogany cabinet with a tinted plaster wall above it; the glass is cleaved to allow a preliminary glimpse of the park before the full view is revealed in the living/dining room. In the gallery space just beyond, a pair of floating burl bookcase/cabinets divide the open space. To the left is the living area, with the dining area to the right and a guest bath beyond. Subdued white walls and dark Brazilian cherry floors underscore the gallery-like openness of the living/dining area. In addition to the freestanding bookcases and pivoting wall dividers, this space is further articulated by specifically designed wooden window grills and built-in cabinetry on the inside wall, all of which are handcrafted like fine furniture. In particular, the wall-hung cabinets are inspired by the floating sculpture boxes of Donald Judd, combined with the simplicity of Shaker furniture, which help to generate both harmony and scale. Fine artists' prints from the 1930s line the wall above the cabinets, continuing the gallery impression while lending a historical counterpoint to the modern design.

Beyond the living room, the remaining space on the park side is devoted to a media room, the master bedroom, and a round master study, which occupies the apartment's northeast corner. The dressing area is separated by a wood slat door, which continues the fine-art furniture feel of the living/dining space. A curved sliding door separates the circular study and sleeping portions of the master bedroom suite. The master bath walls are clad in Bottecino Classico marble and horizontal surfaces of Crema Marfil marble provide a subtle contrast and play of light. The dual-basin lavatory is flanked with full height panels and cabinets of anigre wood. Two children's bedrooms and bath also occupy the apartment's north wing.

The east wing contains the kitchen, a guest bedroom and bath. The main kitchen is composed of two walls of European beech cabinetry, placed opposite to two walls of painted plaster. Wood and plaster areas are contrasted by a series of windows set between piers; a muted light enters the space from an interior courtyard. An informal eating area is contained within the main kitchen.

The completed apartment comfortably combines a sophisticated modern residence within a revered historic building on New York City's Upper West Side. In a city where space, light, and views are highly prized, this apartment achieves all three: vast expanses of uninterrupted space, unimpeded light, and an unsurpassed view of Central Park.

Architecture and Interior Design by

Lee Harris Pomeroy / Architects
Interior Furnishings by:B-Five Studio

Credits

Private Apartment Residence, New York, NY
Architect and Interior Designer: Lee Harris Pomeroy ï Architects, P.C. - Lee Harris Pomeroy, principal-in-charge; Ronald J. Zeytoonian, project architect.
Engineers: Ambrosino, DePinto & Schmieder (mechanical/electrical/plumbing); Superstructures (structural)
Consultants: Audio Video Systems Inc. (A/V); Beth Lochtefeld (code/expediter); Johnson Schwinghammer (lighting);
Furnishings: B-Five Studio
General Contractor: Scott Bavosa Construction Corp.-Jim Scott, president
Sub-contractors: William Erath & Son, Inc. (ceramic tile); Commercial Electrical Contractors Inc. (electrical); Air-Tech Cooling, Inc. (HVAC); SFA Leinoff Inc. (mill-work); Art-In Construction (plaster); Pilato Brothers Plubming & Heating Co., Inc. (plumbing); Jack A. Corcoran Marble Co., Inc. (stone work); Design Painting (wall finishes); Ideal Floors (wood floor);

STRONG COLORS

Size

1.900 sq. ft.

Entry

Art: Frank Stella, published by Tyler Graphics, Mt. Kisco, NY
Glass block: Pittsburgh Corning
Carpet: Rosecore, New York, NY
Paint: Pratt & Lambert

Living Room

Art: The large monoprint on the green wall is by Pierre Aleshinsky.
Rug: Custom made by Elizabeth Browning Jackson.
Table next to black sofa: Constantin, by Simon.
Black sofa: Saladino
Black chair: Philippe Starck
Table in foreground: Noguchi, by Herman Miller
Sofa in foreground: Sity (Citterio), by B&B
Shelves: Nuvola Rosa (Magistretti), by Cassina

Fireplace

Square photograph: by William Wegman from Yancey Richardson Gallery
Photograph on mantle: Doug and Mike Starn
Candle sticks: Richard Meier, by Swid Powell
Mantle: Existing, with new granite.
Artifacts: gathered by our clients during travels through Southeast Asia

Living room / Yellow wall

Art: Sturer
Chairs: Philippe Starck
Black and white decanter: Jonathan Adler
Rug: Elizabeth Browning Jackson
Vase in foreground: from Christian Tortu at Takashimaya

Dining Room

Custom table designed by Stamberg Aferiat, made by John Depp, Inc.
Chairs: Arne Jacobson, through ICF, NY
Rug: Rosecore
Decanter: Venini
Art: Ellsworth Kelly, published by Gemini G.E.L., Los Angeles
Lamp: JerryStyle, NY
Vase/collander: Philippe Starck, by Alessi

Bathroom

Custom cabinetry through Ray Construction. (Maple with stainless steel counters and sink.
Lamp: Artemide
Vase: &D.

SCULPTURED WALL

Size

880 sq. ft.

Furniture

Fireplace: Ian Crofts/NYC
Cabinets: Triangle Cabinets
Sofa: Dialogica/NYC
Chairs: Cassina
Totem lamp: Godley-Schwann
Orange lamp: Artemide
Noguchi table: Herman Miller
Dining table: Dialogica
Dining chairs: Dialogica
Red chair: Peter Stamberg
Blue Venus: In Homage to Yves Klein (but not by Yves Klein)
Art: Barbara Kasten, Robert Mapplethorpe, Botero, Al Held
Lighting: Flos, Alco, CJ Lighting

Electrical: Lutron, Leviton

Finishes: Pratt & Lambert paints, United Ceramic tile
Appliances: SubZero, General Electric, Dacor
Plumbing: Kroin, Kohler, Acorn, Elkay, Just
Contractor: Wildes Construction, 905 West End Avenue, New York NY 10025
Tel. 212-932 1562
Electro-Mechanical Engineer: J.L. Fox Design, 202 Crooked Hill Road, Pearl
River NJ 10965

PROJECT BY PARTS

Size
2.600 sq. ft.
Furniture
Cabinets: Custom by Stamberg Aferiat Architecture, made by Gene Black Cabi-
network
Sofa: Cassina
Chair: ICF/NYC
Large cocktail table: Saladino Furniture
Small cocktail table: Pace
Dining chairs: Dialogica
Art: Louise Nevelson, David Hockney, John Pfahl, Michael David, Anne Lloyd
Lighting: Flos, Edison Price, CJ Lighting
Electrical: Lutron, Leviton
Finishes: Pratt & Lambert paints
Plumbing: Kroin
Bedroom
Cabinets: as above
Ceramic Vases: Jonathan Adler, NYC
Glass bottles: Michael Anchin, NYC
Art: Robert Rauchenberg
Lighting: Ingo Maurer
Bed: Saporiti

Interior Designer
Rene Nelson Interiors, 50 Close Road, Greenwich CT 08631
Tel. 203-661 2910
Contractor: Ray Construction, 309 Passaic Avenue, West Caldwell, NJ 07006
Tel. 973-882 0277

BIOGRAFIE
BIOGRAPHIES

ARCHITECTUREPROJECT LLP
180 Varik Street, New York, NY 10014
Tel.212-6911611-Fax.212-691 2244

ARCHITECTUREPROJECT LLP, founded in 1995 by Mark Janson AIA and Hal Goldstein, AIA, is a full service architectural and interior design firm that specializes in creating high-end residential and retail environments.
The emphasis is on timeless modern design that incorporates materials, textures, and color palettes, which create a feeling of luxurious comfort. The firm custom- designs many of the furnishings and fixtures used in its projects, with an emphasis on classic modern styling.
Clients include Calvin Klein Jeans, for which ARCHITECTUREPROJECT LLP created a new retail image, and The Donna Karan Company, for whom they are creating a new DKNY flagship store on Madison Avenue in Manhattan, as well as the company's first US Collection store to be located at the Americana in Manhasset, New York.
GA Houses and Daidalos have published other residential projects.

The founding partners:
Mark Janson, AIA, was a Senior Associate at Naomi Leff and Associates and an Associate at Steven Holl Architects.
Before co-founding ARCHITECTUREPROJECT LLP he had an independent design studio in New York for a number of years.
His experience includes management of the design and fabrication of numerous major retail and residential projects. Mark studied at the University of Wisconsin and is a graduate of The Parsons School of Design with a Bachelors Degree in Fine Art.
Hal Goldstein, AIA, was Project Architect on a full range of high profile commercial, retail and residential projects at various firms, including Steven Holl Architects and Naomi Leff and Associates before co-founding ARCHITECTUREPROJECT LLP in 1995. He holds a Bachelor of Architecture Degree from Cornell University.

Tamara Beudec, Architect + Atelier
45 Wall Street, Suite 212, New York, NY 10005
Tel.212-3441246-Fax.212-9689891
e-mail: tbeudec@inx.net

Established in 1993, Tamara Beudec Architect + Atelier is a small design-oriented firm based in New York City. The studio pursues rigorous design approaches without adhering to any architectural ideology. In addition to the loft conversion project in Tribeca, the studio has completed several high-end residential interiors in New York City. Since 1997 the studio has been a consultant to Giorgio Armani Fashion Corporation and is involved in assisting its Shop Development group in implementing existing and future store prototypes throughout the USA. The office has launched an independent 'Multy' line of furniture, which consists in single furniture pieces with several configurations, refuting any connection with classifications related to types of furniture. In addition to its New York City projects, the office is currently designing a high-end single family residence in Vermont (USA).
Tamara Beudec was born in Croatia. She received her Bachelor degree from the University of Zagreb in 1986. Several of the university's School of Modern Architecture graduates have become key forerunners and protagonists of the International Style. The ideologies of "machine for living" and "less is more" have greatly influenced Beudec's architectural sensibility. In 1993, while attending Zagreb University, she spent several months in France studying the work of Le Corbusier and she did an internship with the engineering firm 'Technip' in Paris' La Defense. In 1995/96, while still a student, she spent time in Holland studying Dutch architecture and Modern Housing. During that time she did an internship with Rem Koolhas / Office for Metropolitan Architecture in Rotterdam. In 1987 she won a scholarship (teaching assistantship) at Cornell University (1987-89), where she received her Master of Architecture degree. Her graduate design studio work was published in Offramp, an architectural journal published by SCI-Arc in Los Angeles, California. Prior to opening her own studio, she was involved in the development and construction of several high rise office buildings in the USA for the architectural firm Kohn Pedersen Fox Associates P.C. in New York.

Silvia Dainese Architect
Via dei Rogati 1, 35122 Padova; Italy
Tel.049-664908-Fax.049-661186
e-mail: dainese@tin.it

Silvia Dainese was born in 1962.
She earned her degree in architecture in Venice in 1987, studying with Oswald Zoeggler.
From 1987 al 1990 she collaborated on various projects in New York (Gwatmey & Siegel; Transbuilding; Spear & Platt; Asymptote).

In 1990 she began studies at the Directing Film School at N.Y.U.
In 1991 she moved to Italy where she collaborated with the architect P.Bongiana before opening her own studio in Padova.
She is specialized in creating company images and internal architecture.
Her public endeavors include redesigning Piazza Antenore and the Roman St. Lawrence bridge in Padua (currently under construction), as well as the Cortile del Pane inside the Basilica of St. Anthony (currently under construction).
Her design of a 25-unit residential complex in Montebello Vicentino (Vicenza) is presently being built.

Winka Dubbeldam Architect ARCHI-TECTONICS
111 Mercer st.2, New York, NY 10012
Tel.212-226-0303-Fax.212-219-3106
e-mail: wdubb4ny@bway.net

Winka Dubbeldam, President of Archi-Tectonics, NY, is currently an Adjunct Assistant Professor of Architecture at Columbia University in New York City and a Lecturer at the University of Pennsylvania in Philadelphia. She has also taught and lectured at several universities in Europe, the U.S. and Canada.

Her work has been exhibited in solo shows at Form Zero Gallery in Los Angeles, The Kunsthal in Rotterdam and Dessa Gallery in Lublijiana. In the spring of 1999, she will participate in MOMA's "The Unprivate House" and in an upcoming exhibition at the TZ'Art Gallery in New York.

Along with her Monograph published in 1996 by 010 Publishers, Dubbeldam's work has been published in the periodicals Abitare (Italy), A+U (Tokyo), Summa (Buenos Aires), Space (Seoul), World Architecture (London), Interior Design (New York), Archimade (Geneva), Objekt (Amsterdam) and in the books Waterwerk: Visies op steden aan de River (Zwolle 1995), Techno-Fiction (Weimar 1996) and the forthcoming Data/Forms from Thames and Hudson, London.

Her agency Archi-Tectonics, has constructed an art gallery on West Broadway, the new offices for Gear Magazine and renovated several lofts in New York City. She prepared urban planning proposals as consultant to the City Councils of Dordrecht and The Hague in Holland. Her more recent work includes a new Digital Imaging Facility in Midtown Manhattan, a multipurpose building in Brooklyn, a house in upstate New York and a proposal for three residential towers in Rotterdam (in association with Architektenburo Rokus Visser, Rotterdam).

A graduate of the Institute of Higher Education, Faculty of Arts & Architecture, Rotterdam and the Academy of Architecture, Rotterdam, she received a Masters Degree from Columbia University in New York City in 1990. She has previously worked in several offices in Holland, as well as for Bernard Tschumi Architects and Peter Eisenman Architects.

Karen Fairbanks - Scott Marble Architects
66 West Broadway, 600, New York, NY 10007
Tel.212-2330653-Fax.212-2330654
e-mail: kf17@columbia.edu

Karen Fairbanks
Karen Fairbanks is a partner at Scott Marble & Karen Fairbanks Architects.
Prior to this partnership, she was a designer at Cooper Robertson + Partners; Aedificare, Architects; Davis, Brody & Associates; and Graham Gund Associates.
She received her Master of Architecture degree at Columbia University where she won the A.I.A. Medal in 1987, the William Kinne Fellowship in 1987 for her research proposal Japanese Theatrical Space: Body, Movement, Form; the Fred L. Liebman Book Award from the New York Society of Architects in 1986 she and was the representative for Columbia University in the S.O.M. Traveling Scholarship Competition in 1986. She received her Bachelor of Science in Architecture degree from the University of Michigan in 1981.
Karen Fairbanks is currently the Director of the Barnard and Columbia Colleges' Architecture Program and is a full time faculty member of Barnard College, Columbia University. She has been teaching at Columbia University since 1989. Prior to her appointment at Barnard College, she was director of the Columbia College Architecture Program. She has also taught at Parsons School of Design and at the Rensselaer Polytechnic Institute.
She was a fellow of the New York Foundation for the Arts in Architecture in 1988 and 1994. She has served as a panelist for the Architecture Awards for the New York Foundation for the Arts and on the Young Architects Committee for the Architectural League of New York.

Scott Marble
Scott Marble is a partner at Scott Marble & Karen Fairbanks Architects. Prior to entering this partnership, he was a partner in Russ Drinker & Scott Marble Archi-

tects and a designer at Bausman & Gill Associates; Aedificare, Architects; Peter L. Gluck & Partners; and Shepherd & Boyd USA.

He received his Master of Architecture degree from Columbia University in 1986 where he was awarded the A.I.A. Award and the William Kinne Fellowship for his proposal The Architecture of the Algerian Sahara. He received his Bachelor of Environmental Design degree from Texas A&M University in 1983.

Scott has taught at Columbia University's Graduate School of Architecture, Planning, and Preservation since 1987, serving as the Coordinator of Graduate Studies from 1992-1994. He currently teaches at the graduate school. He has been the editor of Abstract, the catalogue of the Graduate School of Architecture, Planning and Preservation of Columbia University, since 1995.
In 1987 he co-edited the book Architecture and Body, published by Rizzoli. Scott was a fellow of the New York Foundation for the Arts in Architecture in 1994. In 1992 he was a winner in the Young Architects Forum sponsored by the Architectural League of New York and he served on the selection committee in 1993.

Gabellini Associates
585 Broadway, New York, NY 10012
Tel.212-3881700-Fax.212-3881808
e-mail: Gabellini@aol.com

Gabellini Associates is recognized for its signature designs based on simplicity of means relative to form and function. The company offers a unique experience in conceptualizing innovative and elemental design solutions for special environments. By complementing light, space and materials with clients' individual needs, Gabellini Associates distills the craft of design into an intuitive art form. In this regard, Gabellini Associates has established itself as an innovator in the field of architectural and interior design.

In 1991, Michael Gabellini founded Gabellini Associates as an architectural and interior design firm. Since its inception, the firm has specialized in fashion boutiques, showroom facilities, exhibition projects, residential and furniture design, as well as in lighting, collaborating with a select international clientele. Clients include Jil Sander, Nicole Farhi, Adrienne Vittadini, Solomon R. Guggenheim Museum and the Council of Fashion Designers of America.
The firm's philosophy is founded on the concept of multi-disciplinary practice. Currently, Gabellini Associates has twenty-five full time employees, including licensed architects, project managers and designers, as well as furniture and sourcing specialists who, together, design, manage and implement projects worldwide. The staff's multilingual skills and comprehensive CADD capabilities enable the office to interface efficiently and productively with our clients worldwide on a diverse range of projects.
Gabellini Associates has received numerous architectural and design awards, including the American Institute of Architects' Medallion Award for the 10,000 sq.ft. Jil Sander Flagship Store and Showroom in Paris. In addition, these awards include the 1998 American Institute of Architects' awards for the Jil Sander Showroom in Hamburg, the Jil Sander and Ultimo boutique in San Francisco, as well as the International Competition for the redesign of Piazza Isolo in Verona.

Gwathmey Siegel & Associates
475 Tenth Avenue, New York, NY 10018
Tel.212-947.1240-Fax.212-9670890
e-mail: c.litherland@Gwathmey-Siegel.com
www.gwathmey-siegel.com

Firm Profile
Transforming problem-solving into art

Thirty years ago in New York City, Charles Gwathmey and Robert Siegel founded what would prove to be an extremely productive and diverse architectural practice. Fresh out of architecture school, Gwathmey was already known for the residence and studio he had designed for his parents in Amagansett, New York. The project remains an iconic point of reference. For Gwathmey, it represents a "pure" architectural intervention, an experience paralleled and consolidated in the firm's design of the Zumikon Residence in Switzerland some twenty-five years later.

From this foundation, Gwathmey and Siegel have gone on to build a prolific office, employing 75 people, whose design portfolio includes libraries, museums and art galleries, colleges and universities, renovations and additions to existing structures, theaters, laboratories, gymnasiums and athletic facilities, hospitals, office buildings, performing arts centers and private residences. The firm has completed more than 300 projects.

In 1982, Gwathmey Siegel & Associates became the youngest firm ever to receive the American Institute of Architects' highest honor: the Firm Award. The citation praised the architects for "approaching every project with a fresh eye, a meticulous attention to detail, a keen appreciation for environmental and economic concerns . . . and a strong belief in collaborative effort." The following year, the AIA's New York Chapter awarded Charles Gwathmey and Robert Siegel the Medal of Honor. The Gwathmey Siegel team has gone on to receive numerous design awards and their accomplishments have won them international recognition.

The partners' pragmatism sets the tone for the office. "What we're really about," says Siegel, "is work and problem-solving." Gwathmey emphasizes the ascendancy of practice over theory: "You can't deny the density of the reality of building." When a new project is undertaken, the architects sit down to brainstorm. Every design is a process of discovery and editing that generates essential composite relationships between object and site, program and form. Every design is developed and worked through together, often over a common table, face to face. Sketches are passed back and forth, notes are made, and details are discussed and debated. The Gwathmey Siegel partnership is not an alliance of artist and technician, nor do the two partners divide the jobs between them; they both design all of the firm's buildings and oversee every project from start to finish, welcoming ideas from both client and project team.

Discussing with the client is an initial and crucial step of the design process. The goal is to create a climate of mutual discovery and collaboration that will persist from the preliminary conceptual phase through final occupancy. Each new endeavor begins with a series of meetings between the client, the two principals and the Associate-in-Charge to determine and refine the program. Once a flexible program has been determined, associates (chosen on the basis of their experience and knowledge of a particular building type) develop the principals' schematic design and govern the daily operations of the team.

Henderson - Sigler STUDIO
39-07 24th Street ,Long Island City, NY,11101
Tel.-Fax.718-3616662
e-mail: porteprato@arthlink.net

Beth Sigler
After studying fine arts at the University of Cincinnati, Ohio, Beth moved to New York to study architecture at the Cooper Union. Since graduating in 1994, she has worked on public architecture projects, several book projects and collaborated with artist Martha Lewis on installations. She has worked as a designer with Weiss and Warchol Studio and Samuel Anderson Architect.

Paul Henderson
After completing a degree in art history at Pitzer College in Claremont, CA, Paul worked in art galleries in Los Angeles. He began to build in 1980, renovating several galleries and building exhibition spaces at the Temporary Contemporary of the Museum of Contemporary Art. He moved to New York in 1985 and worked as project manager on various residential and commercial projects before applying to the Cooper Union in 1988. Since graduating in 1994, he has worked for Anderson/ Schwartz Architects, Anderson Architects and Alliance Builders Corp.

Other joint projects have included the Gussow Studio in Amagansett, NY and the Nickerson/ Wakefield Loft in Manhattan.

Ken Kennedy Architect
10 Mitchell Place 1/B, New York, NY 10017.
Tel.212-7531204-Fax.212-9407580
e-mail:JCURCURR@aol.com

Ken Kennedy, architect, graduated from the University of Technology in Sydney Australia in 1981.
He had a private practice in Australia for ten years, during which time he completed a number of residential and commercial interior commissions that were published in Vogue Living, Belle and Transition. His Guin House, which won a Royal Australian Institute of Architects' merit award in 1996, was included in the book, Sydney, A guide to recent Architecture (Ellipsis Press, London).
He was architectural editor of Monument Magazine from 1994 - 1996.
He also worked in London from 1982 - 1985 as a consultant on graphic and interior design work and won a D&AD merit award in 1984.
He now practices architecture and interior design and lives in New York.

Gerner Kronick + Valcarel, Architects, PC
35 Waterside Plaza New York, NY 10010
Tel.212-679-6362-Fax.212-6795877

Gerner Kronic + Valcarel, Architects, PC, founded in January 1995, is an architecture and design firm with a focus on quality base building and interior design solutions. Its partners, Randolph H. Gerner, AIA, Richard N. Kronick, AIA and Miguel Valcarcel, AIA, have been working together for the past 16 years. Formerly partners with KPF Interior Architects, their expertise ranges from commercial, residential and restoration, to hotels and academic projects. They have worked on projects totaling more than 20 million square feet combined. Some of these projects include: HypoVereinsbank, SFX Entertainment, Bear Stearns & Company, Proctor & Gamble, Viacom, Skytel, Maçka Palace, Garanti Bank Tower, Japan Travel Bureau, El Diario, Fortis Inc., Pall Corporation, Mobile Telecommunication Technologies and EMI Records.

GKV is presently designing a 650,000 sq. Ft. project for Bear Stearns & Company, the 600,000 sq ft. Garanti Bank Headquarters in Istanbul, Turkey, a 25,000 square foot project for SFX Entertainment, MTV, as well as several other projects. In total, the firm is actively engaged in more than two and a half million square feet of design work both in United States and abroad.

Although only four years old, Gerner Kronick + Valcarcel, Architects has received notoriety in numerous publications, including Interiors, Haut Décor, Real Estate Weekly, Interior Design, The New York Times, as well as being published in several new books: Urban Interiors in New York & USA and The New American Apartment.

Richard N. Kronick AIA, and Gerner Kronick & Valcarcel, Architects
Richard Kronick is a founding partner of Gerner Kronick + Valcarcel, Architects, PC. Since the firm's inception in 1995, he has designed more than two million square feet of space. Some of those projects include Hypo Vereinsbank, New York, NY; SFX Entertainment, New York, NY; Doris Duke Charitable Foundation, New York, NY; Fortis Inc., New York, NY; Palmer Lodge, Jackson, Mississippi; Happel Residence, New York, NY; Bear Stearns Headquarters, New York, NY; Ugland House, Grand Cayman, British West Indies; and Slates Showroom, New York, NY Mr. Kronick was formerly a partner with the internationally recognized interior architectural firm KPF Interior Architects, PC. He worked there for over twelve years on projects such as The Equitable Headquarters, New York, NY; MONY Headquarters, New York, NY; Hotel Colon, Guayaquil, Ecuador; Ameritrust Headquarters, Cleveland Ohio, Nationsbank Headquarters, Charlotte, North Carolina; 477 Madison Avenue, New York, NY; and the Palmer Residence, Washington D.C. Mr. Kronick was associated with Gruzen and Partners prior to joining KPF.

228

Mr. Kronick's work has been featured in numerous publications such as the New York Times, Architectural Record, Interior Design, Interiors, Architecture Digest, The New American Apartment, Urban Interiors in New York & USA and Contract Magazine. He has been a participant in numerous round table discussions as well as a guest critic and lecturer at Parson's School of Design and Regis High School. He has also been a guest panelist for industry events at Neocon in Chicago and Designer's Saturday in New York.

Mr. Kronick studied architecture at Ryerson Polytechnical Institute in Toronto, Canada. He is a registered architect in the state of New York and a member of the American Institute of Architects.

Miguel Valcarcel, is one of the three founding partners of Gerner Kronick + Valcarcel, Architects, PC. His expertise in management and technical applications has contributed immensely in establishing GKV as one of the most prestigious new firms. He has been partner-in-charge on such projects as Hypo Vereinsbank, New York City; SFX Entertainment, New York City; Doris Duke Charitable Foundation, New York City; El Diario La Prensa, New York City; Ugland House II, Grand Cayman; Slates Showroom, New York; and Japan Travel Bureau, New York City.

Prior to starting GKV, Mr. Valcarcel was a partner in the internationally recognized firm KPF Interior Architects, PC. He was there for twelve years and worked throughout the world on such projects as 50 Avenue Montaigne, Paris, France; the Federal Reserve Bank of Dallas, Dallas, Texas; NationsBank Corporate Headquarters, Charlotte, North Caroline; Milgrim Thomajan & Lee, New York City; FCB/Leber Katz partners, New York City; MONY Financial Services Headquarters renovation, New York City; The Equitable Headquarters, New York City; and the Justice Center of Buenos Aires at Puerto Madero Programming and Master Plan, Buenos Aires, Argentina. Mr. Valcarcel was associated with the firm Skidmore, Owings and Merrill, Architects before joining KPF.

In addition to participating in several round table discussions and panels, he has been an instructor at the Parson's School of Design. Many of his projects have been featured in publications such as: Interiors, Nikkei, Architectural Record, Building Design & Construction and The New York Times.

Mr. Valcarcel attended the City College of the City University of New York where

he received a Bachelor of Science in Architecture (cum laude). His is a registered architect in the State of New York.

Diane Lewis Architect
11 East 10th St. 2nd fl., New York, NY 10003.
Tel.212-388-0094-Fax.212-3880547

Diane Lewis is a native of New York City where she has maintained an independent studio and has been professor at the Cooper Union Faculty for the past fourteen years.
Her projects in New York City include museums, galleries, houses, offices, parks, film studios, libraries and civic institutions, such as the Basketball Foundation in the South Bronx, the Kunsthalle in New York and the Cooper Union student housing.
The studio projects, both constructed and proposed, have been published internationally in the architectural press. As well, her theoretical writings and essays have been widely published in art and literary journals. Her most recent publication was an essay on post-war New York architecture. She has collaborated as co-editor with Rizzoli on many projects with artists such as Carl Andre, Miralda, Pooh Kaye, Peter Halley, including dance and theatre sets, installations and site coordination for public art installation.
First site architect art on the beach she has been visiting professor in architectural urbanism at Harvard University for a sequence of five years from 1991-95; Yale from 1978-82, 89 and 90 where she conducted studios of artist and architect collaborations.
Visiting scholar of the Architectural Association, London, and lectured and taught in Denmark, Holland, Australia and Austria.
Recipient of the Rome Prize in Architecture in 1976, she also received grants from the Graham Foundation, and the New York State Council on the Arts. Her apprenticeship was conducted over seven years at the offices of Richard Meiwer, and I.M. Pei and Partners.
Having delivered the Hilla Rebay lecture at the Guggenheim Museum 1996, "Distance in the flat", will be part of her forthcoming book, "Rome is the ancient New York".

LOT/EK
55 Little West 12th Street, New York, NY.
Tel./Fax.212-2559326
e-mail: LOTEKARCH@aol.com

LOT/EK is architecture built on the grounds of theoretical experimentation and ingenuity.
LOT/EK is design that integrates electronic, organic and manufactured materials excavated from the contemporary urban landscape.
LOT/EK is customizing the space or object to specific living, work, or play needs of the human bodies, which are to occupy the space or use the object.
LOT/EK is inspired by the evolution of natural and artificial resources, industrial byproducts and high-tech materials as they are woven into the fabric and structures of
everyday life.
LOT/EK is constructing environments for the future on the foundation of our bio-technological-industrial present.
LOT/EK is Ada Tolla and Giuseppe Lignano, graduates of the School of Architecture of the Università di Napoli, Italy (1989) and of post-graduate studies at Columbia University in New York City (1990-91).

Benjamin Noriega-Ortiz Architect
75 Sprin Street, New York, NY 10012
Tel.212-343-9709-Fax.212-3439263

Described by House Beautiful for two consecutive years as one of the "most influential designers" working in America and as a member of the "the next wave of America's 26 best decorators" (November 1998), Benjamin Noriega-Ortiz is unquestionably recognized as one of the most stylistic and influential interior designers today.
Prior to beginning his professional career at John F. Saladino, Inc., where he spent nine years, six of which as Head Designer, Benjamin earned two master degrees in Architecture; one from Columbia University and another from the University of Puerto Rico.
In 1992, Benjamin established his own firm, with projects commissioned by clients such as the New York Times' best selling author Laura Esquivel, fashion designer Steve Fabrikant, media mogul Michael Fuchs, Baccarat Crystal and Kohler.
His work has been featured in a variety of publications, including Architectural Digest, the New York Time Magazine, Metropolitan Home, House Beautiful and Elle Décor, catapulting Benjamin Noriega-Ortiz to the top of his profession

Education:
1974-1979 Master of Science in Architecture and Urban Design, Columbia University, New York
1979-1982 Master in Architecture, University of Puerto Rico
School of Architecture, Puerto Rico
1974-1979 Bachelor in Environmental Design from the University of Puerto Rico School of Architecture, Puerto Rico.

Experience:
Established his own interior design firm in New York City in October 1992
Projects completed: Amcito, Inc.; Rockefeller Center, NY; Baccarat window display, 625 Madison Avenue, New York; Clark/Williams residence, East 93rd Street, NY; Ms. .Marge Nemarrais' residence, West 67th Street, NY; Mr. and Mrs. Alfred Engelberg's residence, Palm Beach, Florida; Laura Esquivel's residence, 9 St. Mark's Place, Westhampton, NY; Steve Fabrikant boutique at Bergdorf Goodman, Bergdorf Goodman, 5th Avenue/57th Street NY; Mr. and Mrs Ron Globerman's residence, Warren, NJ; Mr. Benjamin Jacobson's residence, New York, NY; Kohler display bathroom, National Homebuilder's Show, Houston, Texas and Atlanta,Georgia; Kohler Design Center, Kohler, Wisconsin in celebration of their 125th anniversary in 1998; Mr. And Mrs. David McCourt's residence, 300 Boylston Street, Boston, Mass.; Mr. and Mrs Shuman's residence, New York City, NY; Mr. And Mrs. Stan Smith's residence, East Hampton, NY; Mr. Steven Weber's residence, 50 Central Park West, NY.

1983 - Oct.92 Head interior designer at John F.Saladino, Inc.; interior design and project management of Dr. James W. Smith's medical offices; Schafer Residence, 10 Gracie Square; Chase Bank Private Banking Branch, 64th/Madison; Nutrasweet Headquarters, Deerfield, Ill.; Mr. and Mrs. Norman Lear's residence, Los Angeles, CA.; Mr. and Mrs. Brian Little's residence, Amagansett, NY and Montecito, CA; Diane Woodner's residence, 39 West 67th Street, NY; Regent Hotel, East 57th St, NY and Milan (Now the Four Seasons Hotel).

Parson + Fernandez-Casteleiro, Architects.
62 White Street, New York NY 10013.
Tel.212-4314310-Fax.212-4314496

The confidence and strength of Parson + Fernandez-Casteleiro's designs come from the variety of scales and project types they have experienced and continue to seek out. This variety has resulted in a unique exposure to a large spectrum of materials and construction techniques that in turn has encouraged an extraordinary amount of experimentation. The partners also feel that communication is the key to acceptance of anything new and rely on developing a close dialogue with their clients trough a three step design process. The first steep consist of an analysis of existing conditions, programmatic requirements, site constraints and a thorough examination of the client's needs; The second step consists of the development and review of design options whose viability is also gauged with regard to cost constraints. One of these options is selected and developed into a final design solution during the third step, culminating in a complete architectural statement that may be later documented for construction.

Jeffrey George Parson, AIA
As the Managing Director of the firm, Mr. Parson is responsible for project development and monitoring of all budgets and schedules.
Mr. Parsons' most recent work includes a new garden services building for the Brooklyn Botanic garden, a mile-long urban waterfront park along the Raritan River for the City of New Brunswick, the G.H. Bass regional showroom in New York City, G.H. Bass retail stores in Thailand, Singapore, Philippines, Taiwan and Japan, The Crossroads Theatre, an experimental 300- seat house in New Brunswick, New Jersey, and an addition to the Equitable Life Assurance Company Data Center in New Jersey. In recent years Mr. Parson has directed the design of corporate offices, hotels and laboratories for clients that include Bristol-Myers Squibb, Sterling Drug, Pratt Hotels and Rutgers University. Other projects include a 30-story residential tower in New York City for the Milstein Corporation and Criminal courthouses for Philadelphia and New York as well as several office and residential interiors, and mixed use waterfront developments for private clients.

Marco Pasanella
The Polenta Group Ltd.
285 West Broadway, 200, New York, NY
Tel.212-9650285-Fax.212-9650286
e-mail: Pasanella@aol.com

Marco Pasanella was born in New York City. After graduating from Yale, Marco went on to work as a freelance writer and photographer, working with such publications as Elle, ID and Casa Vogue. In 1988, he was named Contributing Editor at Taxi magazine, where he concentrated on architecture, travel and design. Marco founded The Pasanella Company, a multi-disciplinary design firm, in 1990.

Since then, he has been featured in numerous magazines and newspapers (including 5 times on the cover of The New York Times' Home section), awarded various honors (the Metropolitan Home Design 100, the ID 40, Who's Who in America) and asked to speak at a number of conferences and universities (including the Parsons School of Design, where he teaches in the Interior Design department).
Television appearances include ABC's Good Morning America, Lifetimes' The Wire and the Discovery Channel's Gimme Shelter. Marco had several designs acquired by the Cooper-Hewitt National Design Museum for its permanent collection. Even President Clinton has one of his rockers.

Recent projects include the Sunset Beach Hotel on Shelter Island for Andre Balazs, owner of the Chateau Marmont.
He has also written dozens of magazine articles, including an ongoing column, Decorating for Guys, for Esquire. Marco is also currently finishing a book titled Great Design (for those of us who are neither rich, idle nor handy) to be published by Simon & Schuster in the Spring of 2000.

Giovanni Pasanella, J. Arvid Klein, Henry K. Stolzman, Wayne Berg Architects PC
330 West 42nd Street New York, NY 10036
Tel.212-5942010-Fax.212-9474381
e-mail: info@pksb.com

Pasanella + Klein Stolzman + Berg is an award winning New York City architectural firm with experience in a variety of projects of exceptional design quality. Founded as a small practice in 1964, the firm has grown to employ over 20 architects. PKSB designs public and educational buildings, offices, hospitals and residential interiors.
The firm's current work includes renovations to the Shoreham Hotel in New York, a new dormitory at the Pratt Institute in the children's wing of Brooklyn's Public Library and Mason Hall at SUNY Fredonia. Recent awards include an American Institute of Architects National Honor Award and a 1997 AIA/NYC Design Award.

229

Lee Harris Pomeroy Associates Architects
462 Broadway, New York, NY 10013
Tel.212-3342600-Fax.212-3340093

Education:
Bachelor of Architecture / Rensselaer Polytechnic Institute / 1955
Master of Architecture / Yale University / 1961
Yale Alumni Prize in 1961.

Registrations:
Registered architect in New York, New Jersey, Connecticut, Maine, Massachusetts, Pennsylvania,
Vermont, and Florida.
National Council of Architectural Registration Boards.

Lee Pomeroy founded Lee Harris Pomeroy Associates /Architects in 1964. He leads the firm in the design of a wide range of project types and is an authority in urban design, historic preservation, and New York zoning laws.
In addition to award-winning residential projects, he was architect for the Swiss Bank Tower, HBO Satellite Communications Center, 350 Hudson Street, 375 Hudson Street, New Rochelle Public Library, Ronald McDonald House, Jericho Public Library, Lally School of Management and Technology Rensselaer Polytechnic Institute, Bedford Mews and the reconstruction of Subway Stations at Union Square, Museum of Modern Art, Lincoln Center and Fulton Street.

Mr. Pomeroy was the recipient of a National Endowment for the Arts grant to co-author a plan to save New York's historic Broadway Theater District. His efforts saved the Helen Hayes and Morosco Theaters and led to the designation of many Broadway theaters as landmarks. He is also responsible for major revisions to the city-zoning ordinance. His efforts were recognized by a Municipal Arts Society Award for "raising the consciousness of New Yorkers to their theater heritage".

Prominent among Mr. Pomeroy's preservation projects are the Plaza Hotel, Trinity Church Pedestrian Bridge and Parish House, Saks Fifth Avenue Expansion, Grand Central Terminal, Compton and Goethals Hall at City College of New York, Mystery Point, and 285 Central Park West.

His work has led to recent appointments to several international commissions. In addition, he is responsible for restoring and redesigning eight historic buildings in the heart of Prague, in the Czech Republic, including the luxurious Hotel U Sixtu for the Kempenski Hotel Group. Another luxury hotel, located in Tianjin, in the Peoples' Republic of China, is currently being projected, as is a large-scale master plan for the area.

Smith and Thompson Architects
542 Cathedral Parkway New York, NY 10025
Tel. 212-8650151-Fax.212-8650779

G. Phillip Smith and Douglas Thompson Architects was founded by its two principal partners in 1975. Both are graduates of the Columbia University School of Architecture and Planning. Prior to opening their own offices, Smith worked for Giovanni Pasanella in New York and Maki and Associates in Tokyo, as well as Architects Team Three in Singapore and Penang, Malaysia. Thompson worked for Mitchell/Giurgola architects in New York.
Their work has been exhibited at several institutions in New York, the Guild Hall Museum in east Hampton and at an international traveling exhibit organized by the Art Institute of Chicago. They have also been published in journals and magazines in the Japan, Germany, Italy and the USA.
The firm has won an architectural competition for the East Hampton Airport Terminal, as well as awards for residential projects and, most recently, the AIA award for the Jacques Marchals Museum of Tibetan Art.
Recent projects include facilities for the New York Buddhist Church, the Jacques Marchais Museum, the Italian Language Institute and a new gallery building in the Chelsea art district, as well as numerous residences and corporate interiors.

Stamberg and Aferiat Architecture
126 Fifth Avenue New York, NY 10011
Tel. 212-255-4173-Fax.212-2550149
e-mail: stamafer@aol.com

Paul Aferiat
Paul Aferiat attended Carnegie-Mellon University where he received his Bachelor of Architecture degree (1974.)

Peter Stamberg
Peter Stamberg attended Columbia College, the Rhode Island School of Design and The Architectural Association of London Graduate School of Architecture. He has a Bachelor in Fine Arts (1972), a Bachelor of Architecture (1973) and an AA Graduate Diploma (1975).

Their partnership began in 1976 and Stamberg Aferiat Architecture was founded in 1989. Rizzoli International published a monograph on their work in 1997.

Projects include additions to the Clifty Creek School, Columbus IN; Julie: Artisans' Gallery, New York NY; The Long Island Children's Museum, Garden City NY; Sycamore Creek, Princeton NJ; Salsa Sofa Collection for Knoll International; Persky/Patton House, Shelter Island NY; Hoffman House, East Hampton NY, additions and renovations; Wright Line Showroom, Chicago IL; Loria & Company Gallery, New York, NY; Chiat House, Sagaponack NY; Bradbury/Jones House, East Hampton NY; Persky House, Sag Harbor NY; McCabe & Company Offices, New York NY; Suarez Apartment Renovations, New York NY; Tom and Linda Platt Apartment, New York, NY; Kraus Apartment I, New York NY; Kraus Apartment II, New York NY; Kraus Apartment III, New York NY; Nelson/Sarna Apartment, New York NY, Fisher Apartment, New York NY; Kronick/Shumsky Apartment, New York, NY; Pelletreau & Pelletreau Law Offices, Melville NY.

Studio MORSA
247 Center Street, New York, N.Y 10013
Tel. 212-2264324-Fax.212-9419445

Its two partners, Antonio Morello and Donato Savole established studio MORSA over 25 years ago. The New York based operation has completed projects worldwide, which include retail work at the World Trade Center, lofts in SOHO, shops in Miami Beach and restaurants in Washington D.C., Pasadena and Virginia. The studio is also responsible for a variety of installations in Hokkaido, Japan, the Indies, St. Barthelemy, Spain and Catalunya, as well as for lofts in SOHO and Tribeca in New York City. Morello was educated in Italy and Argentina, while Savoie, an American, was educated in Italy and began his career in New York as an urban designer.

TRI ARCH
42 North Moore Street, New York, N.Y. 10013
Tel. 212-4311455-Fax.212-4311753

Stephen Corelli studied architecture at the University of Toronto, The Architectural Association in London and Princeton University from which he received his M. Arch. Degree in 1983. After working for Michael Graves Architect and Eisenmann/Robertson Architects, Mr. Corelli established his own practice in New York in 1987 in partnership with Michaela Deiss.
Ms. Deiss studied psychology at the University of Lausanne, graduated in Interior Architecture from the "Ecole Des Arts Décoratifs" in Geneva and attended Parson School of Design in New York, from which she obtained an A.A.S. degree in 1984. After collaborating with various architectural firms in Switzerland and New York, Ms. Deiss joined Mr. Corelli in 1987. Their firm, CORELLI/DEISS, completed approximately twenty-five projects between 1987 and 1992. In 1993 they established TRI-ARCH, INC. Since then they have continued to work on a variety of projects types and scales from commercial and high-end residential lofts and apartments to larger scale multi family residential buildings, retail stores, offices and showrooms.
"Developing from a classical concept that views architecture as a public art form, our work incorporates an architectural language inspired by classical architecture and its compositional techniques. We see our creative role in elaborating and transforming this language into new forms that are culturally significant and appropriate to our times".

NUOVI AMBIENTI ITALIANI / *NEW ITALIAN ENVIRONMENTS*

NUOVI NEGOZI A MILANO / *NEW SHOPS IN MILAN*
S. San Pietro - M. Vercelloni

Oltre 15.000 copie vendute in tutto il mondo e 3 ristampe testimoniano il grande successo di questo titolo. 82 negozi milanesi appositamente fotografati per il libro, con testi di commento e schede tecniche dei materiali impiegati e delle aziende che li hanno realizzati.

More than fifteen thousand copies sold world-wide and three reprints are testimony to this book's great success. Photographs of eighty-two Milanese shops are accompanied by commentaries and technical tables, specifying the materials used and the firms responsible for their construction.

1988 (3ª ristampa 1990), 210 x 297, 250 pp., 418 ill. col., testo italiano/inglese.
€ **77,90 / L. 150.000** (brossura/paperback)   ISBN 88-7685-047-3

1

NUOVI NEGOZI IN ITALIA / *NEW SHOPS IN ITALY*
S. San Pietro - M. Vercelloni

Selezione di 86 inediti e prestigiosi negozi italiani, illustrati da foto appositamente realizzate, con testi di commento e schede tecniche con gli indirizzi dei fornitori e le specifiche dei materiali impiegati. Strumento indispensabile, vendutissimo ancora oggi.

Eighty-six selected, unpublished Italian shops, especially photographed for this book, are accompanied by commentaries, technical tables and the names and addresses of the firms responsible for their construction, along with the specifications of the materials used. An indispensable tool, still widely sold today.

1990 (2° ristampa 1993), 210 x 297, 288 pp., 400 ill. col., testo italiano/inglese.
€ **77,90 / L. 150.000** (rilegato/hardback)   ISBN 88-7685-032-5

2

1990. STADI IN ITALIA / *STADIUMS IN ITALY*
S. San Pietro - M. Vercelloni

I 12 eccezionali stadi di calcio dei Mondiali di Italia 90 documentati da un ricchissimo apparato iconografico con disegni e modelli, foto di cantiere e foto appositamente realizzate delle architetture ultimate. Testi critici e di progetto. Antologia d'immagini e appunti per una storia di stadi, circhi e anfiteatri. In appendice normative, standard e sicurezza negli stadi; regolamento italiano e F.I.F.A. del calcio.

The twelve exceptional soccer stadiums of the World Cup Soccer championship, held in Italy in 1990, are documented by a very rich iconography of drawings, models, building yards and completed projects photographs. Critical and descriptive texts accompany the anthology of images and notes of this historical survey on stadiums, circus- and amphitheaters. The appendix contains the regulations, standards and stadium safety, along with the F.I.F.A. and Italian soccer regulations.

1990, 210 x 297, 460 pp., 800 ill. di cui 340 a col., testo italiano/inglese.
€ **93,40 / L. 180.000** (rilegato/hardback)   ISBN 88-7685-024-4

3

GRAND HOTEL IN ITALIA / *GRAND HOTELS IN ITALY*
S. San Pietro - M. Vercelloni

I 20 più significativi grand hotel italiani in città, al mare e in montagna. I testi affiancano spettacolari ed esclusive immagini fotografiche, sottolineando aspetti progettuali e architettonici; le schede tecniche offrono informazioni dettagliate sui materiali impiegati e sugli aspetti funzionali; un accurato profilo descrive i servizi offerti dai grand hotel proponendo il volume anche come utile guida.

Twenty of the most significant grand hotels in Italy, located in cities, seaside and mountain resorts are contained within this book. The texts accompanying the spectacular and exclusive photographs emphasize the design and architectural aspects. The technical tables offer detailed information on the material used and the functional aspects. An accurate profile describes the services offered by the hotels, rendering this volume a useful guide.

1992, 210 x 297, 256 pp., 339 ill. col., testo italiano/inglese.
€ **93,40 / L. 180.000** (rilegato/hardback)   ISBN 88-7685-043-0

4

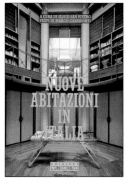

NUOVE ABITAZIONI IN ITALIA / *URBAN INTERIORS IN ITALY*
S. San Pietro - M. Casamonti

Proponendosi come concreto riferimento sulle tematiche dell'abitare sempre in bilico tra desiderio e funzionalità, il libro offre un panorama eterogeneo di 22 recenti interni urbani di altrettanti architetti italiani di fama internazionale. Lettura locale per locale attraverso testi e immagini di grande formato, dettagliate schede tecniche con materiali e fornitori.

This book offers a varied perspective on the issue of a living style that is continually poised between pleasure and functionality. The 22 projects presented here are of urban interiors designed by internationally acclaimed Italian architects. It features detailed commentaries with large pictures and technical tables, which indicate materials used and suppliers.

1993, 210 x 297, 240 pp., 242 ill. col., testo italiano/inglese.
€ **93,40 / L. 180.000** (rilegato/hardback)   ISBN 88-7685-056-2

5

EDIZIONI L'ARCHIVOLTO - via marsala 3 20121 milano - tel 0039.02.29010444 29010424 - fax 0039.02.29001942 - archivolto@homegate.it

NUOVI AMBIENTI ITALIANI / *NEW ITALIAN ENVIRONMENTS*

NUOVI NEGOZI A MILANO 2 / *NEW SHOPS IN MILAN 2*
S. San Pietro - P. Gallo

46 recentissime architetture di importanti negozi milanesi e di differenti merceologie presentate in modo molto scenografico grazie alle splendide fotografie di grande formato che permettono di apprezzare meglio anche i dettagli. Testi critico-descrittivi spiegano i progetti anche attraverso disegni e schede tecniche con informazioni sui materiali e le tecniche impiegate.

Forty-six important and recently built Milanese shops of various kinds, are presented in a very picturesque manner, thanks to the large, splendid photographs, which provide a better understanding of the details. Critical and descriptive texts provide explanations, while drawings and technical tables specify the techniques and materials used.

1994, 210 x 297, 228 pp., 285 ill. col., testo italiano/inglese.
€ **77,90 / L. 150.000** (rilegato/hardback)   ISBN 88-7685-068-6

6

NUOVI NEGOZI IN ITALIA 2 / *NEW SHOPS IN ITALY 2*
S. San Pietro - P. Gallo

L'aggiornatissima documentazione proposta in questo volume analizza la progettazione e l'allestimento di 52 nuovi negozi di differenti merceologie, presentati da testi critici e da straordinarie immagini di grande formato. Disegni di progetto e schede tecniche chiariscono le soluzioni adottate specificando tecniche, materiali impiegati e aziende coinvolte.

The current volume analyzes the design and arrangement of fifty-two new shops of various sorts, accompanied by critiques and large extraordinary images. Project drawings and technical tables clarify the chosen solutions, specifying the techniques and materials used and the names of the architectural firms.

1994, 210 x 297, 260 pp., 331 ill. col., testo italiano/inglese.
€ **77,90 / L. 150.000** (rilegato/hardback)   ISBN 88-7685-069-4

7

VETRINE A MILANO / *WINDOW DISPLAYS IN MILAN*
S. San Pietro

Primo volume veramente esauriente edito in Italia: 170 esempi di vetrine dei più famosi negozi milanesi suddivisi per vie e di differenti merceologie, presentati in modo molto scenografico grazie alle splendide grandi immagini tutte a colori realizzate appositamente. Ogni vetrina ha una dettagliata scheda tecnica con informazioni riguardanti progettisti, vetrinisti, materiali, tecniche e artigiani che le hanno realizzate. In appendice un preziosissimo repertorio di indirizzi di progettisti, vetrinisti e fornitori. Due capitoli sono dedicati agli allestimenti per Natale e alla manifestazione "Futurshop-Progetto Vetrina" (Fiera di Milano).

The first complete volume on this subject published in Italy, it contains 170 samples of display windows of the most famous shops in Milan. They are categorised according to address and type of merchandise and are artistically presented, thanks to the especially created pictures. Technical tables for each picture contain information on the designers, artisans, window dressers and the materials and techniques used in creating each window. The appendix contains an invaluable index of the designers, window dressers and suppliers. One chapter is specifically dedicated to Christmas, while another chapter is dedicated to the "Futurshop-Progetto Vetrina", held at the Milan fairgrounds.

1995, 210 x 297, 260 pp., 170 ill. col., testo italiano/inglese.
€ **77,90 / L. 150.000** (rilegato/hardback)   ISBN 88-7685-074-0

8

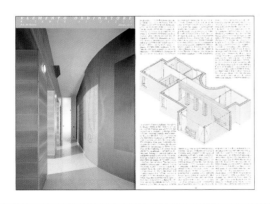

NUOVE ABITAZIONI IN ITALIA 2 / *URBAN INTERIORS IN ITALY 2*
S. San Pietro - M. Vercelloni

Dopo la fortunata apparizione nel 1993 del primo volume (6.000 copie vendute) ecco finalmente il secondo che completa con altre e più recenti realizzazioni il primo. 21 nuovi ambienti urbani di famosi architetti italiani letti locale per locale con immagini tutte a colori e di grande formato. Testi rivolti anche a un pubblico non specializzato, disegni, piante e schede tecniche con dettagliate informazioni su materiali, tecniche e artigiani impiegati per le realizzazioni, descrivono approfonditamente ogni appartamento.

After the initial success of the first volume in 1993 (6.000 copies sold), this second volume completes the first by providing more recent projects. A room-by-room analysis of the 21 urban interiors designed by internationally renowned architects is embellished by large, color photographs. Texts are written in laymen's terms and drawings, plans and a technical table containing detailed information on materials, techniques and the artisans involved are also included.

1995, 210 x 297, 256 pp., 250 ill. col., testo italiano/inglese.
€ **93,40 / L. 180.000** (rilegato/hardback)   ISBN 88-7685-075-9

9

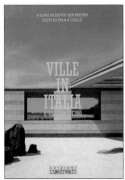

VILLE IN ITALIA E CANTON TICINO / *VILLAS IN ITALY & CANTON TICINO*
S. San Pietro - P. Gallo

Decimo volume della collana, l'opera individua 16 ville al mare, in campagna, in montagna, sui laghi o sui fiumi particolarmente curate nell'architettura anche degli interni. Sono prese in considerazione sia nuove realizzazioni, sia ristrutturazioni e ampliamenti di rustici già esistenti. Dal Canton Ticino a Pantelleria, dalla Brianza alla Liguria e alla Toscana, dal Lazio alla Puglia, per tutte il comune denominatore è la grande qualità degli interventi eseguiti, il particolare contesto del verde in cui si calano, con parchi, giardini e piscine e la varietà tipologica delle loro architetture.

The tenth volume in the series, this book discusses sixteen seaside, country, mountain, lakeside and riverside villas wich are characterized by carefully designed architectures and interiors. New constructions, as well as restorations and expansions of existing country homes are included. From the Canton Ticino to Pantelleria, from Brianza to Liguria and Tuscany, from Lazio to Puglia, the common trait is the fine precision and quality of the work, as well as the particular landscapes in which these willas are located. They illustrate a variety of architectures that include parks, gardens and swimming pools.

1995, 210 x 297, 232 pp., 312 ill. col., testo italiano/inglese.
€ **77,90 / L. 150.000** (rilegato/hardback)   ISBN 88-7685-076-7

10

NUOVI AMBIENTI ITALIANI / *NEW ITALIAN ENVIRONMENTS*

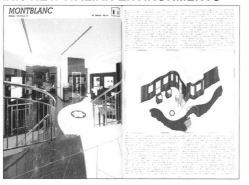

NUOVI NEGOZI IN ITALIA 3 / *NEW SHOPS IN ITALY 3*
S. San Pietro - P. Gallo

Immagini a colori di grande formato, dettagliate schede tecniche, disegni di progetto, repertori con note sui progettisti nonché i realizzatori coinvolti in ciascun intervento costituiscono, insieme ai testi critico-descrittivi, il complesso apparato che guida alla lettura degli ambienti anche milanesi presentati in questo volume, che fa parte di una fortunata serie dedicata alla progettazione di negozi e spazi commerciali. Il libro vuole essere un osservatorio sulla realtà e costituisce una ricca fonte di documentazione e di aggiornamento per architetti, designer, operatori del settore o anche per chi voglia cogliere le ultime tendenze.

The latest volume in this series dedicated to stores and commercial environments, this book is a guide to new spaces including some in Milan. It is characterized by large color photographs, detailed technical tables and floor plans, as well as information on the designers and architectural firms. The book wants to provide facts and it is a perfect source of information for architects, designers and professionals involved in the field, but also for anyone who wants to keep updated on the latest trends.

1995, 210 x 297, 260 pp., 363 ill. col., testo italiano/inglese.
€ 77,90 / L. 150.000 (rilegato/hardback)   ISBN 88-7685-077-5

11

NUOVI ALLESTIMENTI IN ITALIA / *NEW EXHIBITS IN ITALY*
S. San Pietro

Il volume corredato da grandi immagini a colori, presenta 37 significativi allestimenti di mostre culturali, esposizioni, fiere e manifestazioni di vari settori progettati da noti architetti. L'accurata selezione dei progetti, operata unicamente secondo criteri qualitativi, conferisce al libro il valore di un importante documento sull'architettura d'interni e in particolare su realizzazioni destinate, per loro natura, a essere effimere. I commenti critici, le schede tecniche dettagliate, i nominativi dei realizzatori e dei produttori coinvolti lo rendono anche valido strumento di lavoro per i professionisti del settore.

The large colour pictures in this volume illustrate a series of important designs by well-known architects, of cultural exhibitions, shows, trade fairs, and events of various kinds. The projects were selected solely on the basis of their standards of quality, making the book a valuable source of information on interior design, but most particularly on projects destined to be short-lived by their very nature. The commentaries, detailed technical descriptions and information regarding the contractors and manufacturers involved will also make it useful to professionals in the sector.

1996, 210 x 297, 240 pp., 339 ill. col., testo italiano/inglese.
€ 93,40 / L. 180.000 (rilegato/hardback)   ISBN 88-7685-084-8

12

DISCODESIGN IN ITALIA / *DISCODESIGN IN ITALY*
S. San Pietro - C. Branzaglia

Immagini imprevedibili, tutte a colori e di grande formato accompagnano il lettore in un viaggio ricco di sorprese nel variegato mondo italiano della notte. Il volume, corredato di testi descrittivi, di note tecniche e dettagliati apparati, presenta ventiquattro discoteche che fanno tendenza all'insegna della fantasia più sfrenata. È il regno dell'eccesso, del kitsch e degli effetti speciali: uno spaccato sociologico sulla realtà del divertimento notturno italiano, caso unico al mondo. La più completa e complessa rassegna di stili mescolati senza pudore per ottenere atmosfere capaci di varcare la soglia del senso comune.

Surprising images, all in color and large format, accompany the reader on a journey full of surprises through the variegated world of Italian nightlife. The volume, which includes descriptive texts, technical notes, and detailed information, presents twenty-four trendsetting discotheques were the imagination has been allowed to run riot. It is a tour of the kingdom of excess, kitsch, and special effects. A sociological cross section through the reality of nightlife in Italy, a phenomenon with no parallels in the world. It is the most complete and intricate survey of styles, shamelessly blended to create atmospheres capable of surpassing the boundaries of common sense.

1996, 210 x 297, 240 pp., 293 ill. col., testo italiano/inglese.
€ 93,40 / L. 180.000 (rilegato/hardback)   ISBN 88-7685-085-6

13

NUOVI NEGOZI IN ITALIA 4 / *NEW SHOPS IN ITALY 4*
S. San Pietro - P. Gallo

Un'ampia e aggiornatissima panoramica dei nuovi ambienti commerciali realizzati in Italia con l'inserimento, per la prima volta in questa fortunata collana, anche di alcune importanti realizzazioni all'estero firmate da architetti e aziende italiani. Le immagini a colori e di grande formato sono corredate da un ricco apparato costituito da testi critici, dettagliate schede tecniche, disegni di progetto e appendici che segnalano i nominativi di progettisti, aziende, artigiani e fornitori coinvolti nella realizzazione di ciascun intervento e guidano alla lettura degli allestimenti fornendo una documentazione puntuale e di immediata utilità.

A broad and extremely up-to-date panorama of the new commercial interiors that are being produced in Italy, with the inclusion, for the first time in this popular series, of a number of important projects carried out by Italian architects and firms abroad. The large-scale color illustrations are accompanied by critical texts, detailed technical descriptions, plans, drawings and appendices giving the names of the designers, firms, craftsmen and suppliers involved in each intervention and offering a guide to the interpretation of the designs through a precise documentation that will prove immediately useful.

1997, 210 x 297, 260 pp., 339 ill. col., testo italiano/inglese.
€ 93,40 / L. 180.000 (rilegato/hardback)   ISBN 88-7685-096-1

14

LOFTS IN ITALY
S. San Pietro - P. Gallo

Loft indica, nell'accezione americana, un unico grande ambiente destinato in origine ad attività industriali riconvertito poi in abitazione o spazio di lavoro. Progressivamente questo termine ha assunto significati più ampi definendo non solo un fenomeno che ha radici nella realtà del contesto urbano statunitense ma anche spazi molto più eterogenei di luoghi dismessi e legati a una successiva trasformazione d'uso nella costante ricerca di un modo di abitare e lavorare alternativo. Gli esempi proposti - abitazioni, studi d'artisti e uffici - testimoniano la poliedricità contemporanea del fenomeno in Italia, una moda che dura ormai da dieci anni.

The term "loft" refers to any large factory, warehouse, or workshop space that is converted for use as living accomodation or other new activity. In time the expression has acquired a broader meaning, passing from the specifics of American urban situations to a more general use of industrial space that has been refurbished, in the constant pursuit of new modes of living and working. This presentation showcases examples of loft conversions - homes, professional workshops, and even offices - attesting to the sheer diversity of the phenomenon here in Italy, a trend that has been in vogue for ten years now.

1998, 210 x 297, 250 pp., 320 ill. col., testo italiano/inglese.
€ 93,40 / L. 180.000 (rilegato/hardback)   ISBN 88-7685-099-6

15

EDIZIONI L'ARCHIVOLTO - via marsala 3   20121 milano - tel 0039.02.29010444   29010424 - fax 0039.02.29001942 - archivolto@homegate.it

NUOVI AMBIENTI ITALIANI / *NEW ITALIAN ENVIRONMENTS*

NEW SHOPS 5 MADE IN ITALY
S. San Pietro - P. Gallo

Questo libro, documentando le più recenti tendenze che riguardano la progettazione di spazi commerciali, quasi inevitabilmente travalica i confini nazionali testimoniando come "le immagini" del commercial landscape siano analoghe a Milano e a New York, a Beirut come a Tokyo secondo una tendenza che progressivamente supera le specificità locali per identificare modalità espressive e di comunicazione dal carattere internazionale. Accanto ai testi che aiutano a interpretare gli esempi presentati e a ricche appendici, immagini di grande formato e qualità fanno sì che il libro divenga uno strumento di consultazione e uno straordinario repertorio di immediata e grande utilità.

Since this book presents the most recent trends in the planning of retail space, its contents are almost inevitably bound to ignore national boundaries, demonstrating how commercial landscapes are essentially the same in Milan, New York, Beirut and Tokyo. There is, in fact, a clear tendency to go beyond the constraints imposed by the local tradition, opting for more expressive and communicative techniques of an international character. The accompanying texts provide an interpretation of the examples presented, coupled with large format pictures and a detailed appendix. The book can, therefore, be used as a reference, providing an immediate repository of information

1998, 210 x 297, 292 pp., 320 ill. col., testo italiano/inglese.
€ 93,40 / L. 180.000 (rilegato/hardback)   ISBN 88-7685-101-1

16

RENOVATED HOUSES / *CASE RINNOVATE*
S. San Pietro - P. Gallo

Una ricerca inconsueta caratterizza questo volume che affronta il tema, poco indagato in modo sistematico, del rinnovamento di costruzioni extraurbane preesistenti. L'idea sottesa ai progetti selezionati presuppone la rivitalizzazione del passato più che la sua conservazione e ciò indirizza verso la vivace e creativa sperimentazione di tutte le potenzialità - tecniche, materiche e linguistiche - offerte dell'architettura contemporanea. L'identità precisa delle realizzazioni qui riprodotte attraverso immagini di alta qualità è sempre il frutto di una ricerca che assume il passato come componente del nuovo avvalorando l'idea che la storia sia sempre storia contemporanea.

This new book is characterized by an unusual study of renovated suburban homes, a topic that has been researched very little. The project's philosophy presupposes a recollection of the past rather than a true preservation of it, allowing a vibrant and creative experimentation of the techniques, materials and linguistic expression offered by modern architecture. The identity of the creations that are reproduced here, is the result of a study based on the notion that the past is a component of the new. In this way, history is viewed as a modern recounting, a contemporary history.

1999, 210 x 297, 240 pp., 390 ill. col., testo italiano/inglese.
€ 93,40 / L. 180.000 (rilegato/hardback)   ISBN 88-7685-107-0

17

ITALIAN DESIGN

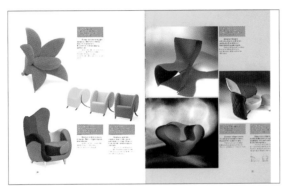

MOBILI ITALIANI CONTEMPORANEI
CONTEMPORARY ITALIAN FURNITURE
C. Morozzi, S. San Pietro - Prefazione di A. Mendini

Oltre 1000 pezzi di produzione italiana, creati da designer italiani e stranieri, illustrati con immagini tutte a colori, documentano la storia del mobile dal 1985 al 1995. Suddiviso in sette sezioni, corrispondenti alle diverse tipologie, con testi storico-critici e prefazione di Alessandro Mendini, colma una lacuna nell'editoria di settore presentandosi come esauriente repertorio, ma anche come strumento di riflessione sui movimenti e sulle tendenze degli ultimi anni. Una dettagliata storia per immagini, con esaustive didascalie di ogni pezzo. Indici e indirizzi dei progettisti e delle aziende.

Over one thousand pieces created in Italy by Italian and foreign designers. Large color illustrations trace the history of furniture from 1985 to 1995. It is divided into seven sections according to distinct typologies and the accompanying texts provide an historical and critical commentary of the period and the evolution of furniture. Alessandro Mendini's introduction mediates the lack of publications in this field, presenting not only an exhaustive range of examples, but also a reflection on the latest shifts and trends. It provides an illustrated history with detailed information on each piece, as well as an index with addresses of the designers and companies.

1996, (2ª ristampa 1999), 240 x 297, 260 pp., oltre 1000 ill. col., testo italiano/inglese.
€ 98,60 / L. 190.000 (rilegato/hardback)   ISBN 88-7685-087-2

1

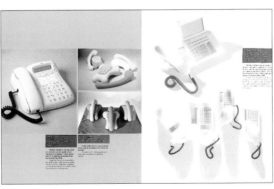

PRODOTTO INDUSTRIALE ITALIANO CONTEMPORANEO
CONTEMPORARY ITALIAN PRODUCT DESIGN
A. Scevola, S. San Pietro - Prefazione di G. Giugiaro

Con prefazione di Giorgetto Giugiaro, l'opera affronta in modo organico e sistematico un tema trascurato dall'editoria. Oltre seicento oggetti italiani o disegnati da progettisti italiani per produzioni straniere, selezionati in relazione all'innovazione tipologica, tecnologica o dei materiali impiegati. Le didascalie dei prodotti permettono di individuarne le caratteristiche e i dettagli tecnici. Cinque grandi sezioni tematiche con testi introduttivi che evidenziano la relazione tra progetto, problemi e sinergie della produzione. Rivolto a progettisti, aziende e a operatori di settori molto diversificati.

With an introduction by Giorgetto Giugiaro, this work represents a systematic picture of a subject hitherto neglected by publishers. The over 600 objects presented have been produced in Italy or created by Italian designers for foreign manufacturers and they have been specifically selected on the basis of their innovative techniques and materials. The characteristics and details of each product are specified. Divided into five sections, the book's introductory texts discuss the relationship between production design, problems and synergy. Aimed at designers, and operators from diversified fields.

1999, 240 x 297, 240 pp., oltre 600 ill. col., testo italiano/inglese.
€ 98,60 / L. 190.000 (rilegato/hardback)   ISBN 88-7685-088-0

2

EDIZIONI L'ARCHIVOLTO - via marsala 3   20121 milano - tel 0039.02.29010444   29010424 - fax 0039.02.29001942 - archivolto@homegate.it

INTERNATIONAL ARCHITECTURE & INTERIORS

1

URBAN INTERIORS IN NEW YORK & USA
Testi di M. Vercelloni - Fotografie di P. Warchol - A cura di S. San Pietro

Dalla tradizione tutta americana del loft, ai lussuosi palazzi newyorkesi degli anni '20 su Central Park, da interventi in architetture simbolo, come le torri di Chicago di Mies van der Rohe, alla vecchia Centrale di Polizia di New York, trasformata in esclusivo condominio. Lo stimolante confronto tra i diversi progetti, il loro grado di approfondimento compositivo e i variegati impieghi materici compongono una eterogenea e straordinaria tavolozza che si inserisce nella ricca e fondamentale tradizione della ricerca architettonica americana sulla casa privata di abitazione. Concludono il volume le biografie dei progettisti e le schede descrittive di ogni progetto.

From the wholly American tradition of the loft to the luxurious New York townhomes of the twenties, overlooking Central Park, and from the restructuring of such architectural symbols as Mies van der Rohe's Chicago skyscrapers to the old central police station in New York, converted into a condominium, this book provides a stimulating comparison of projects. The thought that has gone into their composition and the variety of materials used present a heterogeneous and extraordinary picture, which is in line with the rich and fundamental tradition of American architectural research on private homes. Biographies of the designers and descriptions of each project are included.

1996 (1ª ristampa 1999), 230 x 297, 232 pp., 242 ill. col. + 51 b/n, testo inglese/italiano.
€ 93,40 / L. 180.000 (rilegato/hardback)   ISBN 88-7685-086-4

2

NEW AMERICAN HOUSES. SEA, COUNTRY & CITIES
Testi di M. Vercelloni - Fotografie di P. Warchol - A cura di S. San Pietro

I diciannove progetti di case unifamiliari selezionati per questo libro offrono un diretto approfondimento del discorso iniziato col primo volume della collana sugli appartamenti, sia per il sinergico confronto di linguaggi e figure, differenti poetiche e percorsi progettuali proposti, sia per l'arco di tempo esaminato (l'ultimo decennio), sia soprattutto per il medesimo autore dei servizi fotografici. Le foto sono corredate da ricchi apparati iconografici composti da piante, sezioni, disegni di particolari costruttivi. La descrizione dei materiali è riportata a conclusione del volume con le biografie dei progettisti.

The nineteen homes discussed in this book offer a deeper understanding of the discussion that was begun in the first volume in the series on apartments. The discussion continues with a comparison of both, language and form, as well as of the different pathways that have guided the projects. In addition, the time period being discussed is also the same (the last decade) as are the author and the photographer. The pictures contain rich iconographic explanations that include blueprints, sections and construction details. A list of materials used is provided at the back of the book, along with the designer's biography.

1997, 230 x 297, 232 pp., 259 ill. col. + 113 b/n, testo testo inglese/italiano.
€ 93,40 / L. 180.000 (rilegato/hardback)   ISBN 88-7685-097-X

3

NEW RESTAURANTS IN USA & EAST ASIA
Testi di M. Vercelloni - Fotografie di P. Warchol - A cura di S. San Pietro

I trentasei progetti selezionati realizzati in America, Giappone e Malesia nell'ultimo decennio sono firmati nella quasi totalità da progettisti americani, a esclusione di alcuni locali realizzati in Giappone dall'inglese Nigel Coates e dall'irachena Zaha Hadid. Si tratta quindi di un confronto tra progetti appartenenti alla cultura occidentale e a quella americana in particolare, dove, a differenza che in Europa, l'architettura del ristorante si spinge oltre il semplice progetto d'interni, per abbracciare la dimensione scenografica e spettacolare in cui sperimentare, a volte in totale libertà, nuovi linguaggi e brillanti soluzioni compositive.

This book focuses on restaurants design, offering a broad and stimulating array of thirty-six designs realized over the last decade in the United States, Japan, and Malaysia. The restaurants we have chosen are nearly all designed by North American architects, except for a number of local ones in Japan done by the British Nigel Coates and the Iraqi Zaha Hadid. The book offers a comparative overview of the new western architecture, particulary of the kind emerging in the U.S., where, unlike in Europe, restaurant design involves not just the interiors but the building's entire setting, sometimes allowing total freedom to experiment new languages and imaginative layout solutions.

1998, 230 x 297, 240 pp., 257 ill. col. + 60 b/n, testo testo inglese/italiano.
€ 93,40 / L. 180.000 (rilegato/hardback)   ISBN 88-7685-098-8

4

NEW OFFICES IN USA
Testi di M. Vercelloni - Fotografie di P. Warchol - A cura di S. San Pietro

Questo libro vuole proporre al lettore un panorama aggiornato sul divenire del paesaggio interno dell'ufficio americano, sulle figure chiamate a definire funzioni e percorsi, sui diversi modi di affrontare il progetto d'interni per spazi di lavoro qualificati che non devono più solo rispondere a esigenze quantitative e di semplice funzionamento razionale-distributivo. Tutti gli uffici sono corredati da disegni di progetto e schede tecniche con descrizione di materiali e arredi, note dei progettisti sulle soluzioni adottate negli specifici progetti e loro biografie aggiornate.

The aim of this book is to provide an update on the evolving interior landscape of the American office, the stylistic models used in defining functions and distribution and the different ways of approaching an interior design project aimed at providing quality spaces. This involves more than merely responding to quantitative and logical functional needs. All the offices presented are accompanied by descriptions, as well as by technical data that list the materials and furniture and the designers' notes on the solutions used. The designers' biographies are also included.

1998, 230 x 297, 236 pp., 255 ill. col. + 54 b/n, testo inglese/italiano.
€ 93,40 / L. 180.000 (rilegato/hardback)   ISBN 88-7685-100-3

5

NEW SHOWROOMS & ART GALLERIES IN USA
Testi di M. Vercelloni - Fotografie di P. Warchol - A cura di S. San Pietro

Il volume raccoglie ventisette progetti di showrooms, gallerie d'arte, allestimenti significativi, piccoli musei e ristrutturazioni di musei anche famosi come il Whitney Museum of American Art di New York, dalla fine degli anni '80 ad oggi. I progetti selezionati, per lo più inediti e mai raccolti sistematicamente come in questo caso, offrono un composito e ricco scenario sull'architettura degli spazi "per esporre" made in Usa. Testi descrittivi accompagnano tutti i progetti, corredati anche da disegni. Concludono il volume le biografie dei progettisti e le schede descrittive di materiali e soluzioni tecniche riferite ai progetti selezionati.

The present volume showcases twenty-seven projects that include showrooms, art galleries, installations, small museums and modernization schemes for internationally renowned museums, such as the Whitney Museum of American Art in New York, all realized in the United States from the end of the 1980's. The projects have never been published or systematically collected in this way. They offer an excellent view into the rich architecture of 'exposition' spaces in the USA. Each project is accompanied by a detailed description. Biographies of the designers and technical charts are included.

1999, 230 x 297, 224 pp., 228 ill. col. + 63 b/n, testo inglese/italiano.
€ 93,40 / L. 180.000 (rilegato/hardback)   ISBN 88-7685-102-X

INTERNATIONAL ARCHITECTURE & INTERIORS

LOFTS & APARTMENTS IN NYC
Testi di M. Vercelloni - Fotografie di P. Warchol - A cura di S. San Pietro

Altri venticinque straordinari progetti di nuovi spazi domestici newyorkesi, realizzati dalla fine degli anni '80 a oggi, raccolti in un efficace confronto che offre un composito e ricco scenario sui nuovi modi d'intendere l'abitare e di vivere la casa, sia dal punto di vista funzionale e distributivo, sia per quanto riguarda l'immagine architettonica e l'atmosfera degli interni. Il 'tipo' del loft, spazio industriale newyorkese per eccellenza, impiegato negli anni '60 dagli artisti di Soho come ineguagliabile casa-laboratorio, si confronta con una serie di nuovi esclusivi appartamenti, di abitazioni per collezionisti d'arte e di fotografia.

Another twenty-five extraordinary new projects of New York living spaces, created between the end of the 80's and the present, and collected in a way that allows easy comparisons, offering a rich perspective on new living styles from both, a functional and a distributive point of view. It also provides insight on the architectural imagery and atmosphere of the interiors. The loft, the New York-style industrial space converted for residential use, originally used by Soho artists in the 60's as an incomparable home-lab, has been converted into exclusive apartments, providing living space for art and photography collectors.

1999, 230 x 297, 240 pp., 259 ill. col. + 36 b/n, testo inglese/italiano.
€ 93,40 / L. 180.000 (rilegato/hardback)   ISBN 88-7685-104-6

6

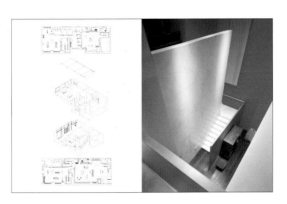

NEW STORES IN USA
Testi di M. Vercelloni - Fotografie di P. Warchol - A cura di S. San Pietro

Ventinove progetti di negozi e boutiques, tutti realizzati negli Stati Uniti dall'inizio degli anni '90 ad oggi, si confrontano in questo libro configurando uno scenario eclettico e composito. Gli interni commerciali selezionati coprono un panorama che raccoglie negozi di tendenza e punti vendita più tradizionali, spazi rivolti a un pubblico più vasto e nuove esclusive boutiques. Significativi allestimenti, a volte paragonabili a vere e proprie gallerie d'arte, che offrono una stimolante e ricca rassegna sull'architettura del negozio made in Usa. Ogni progetto è stato fotografato da Paul Warchol, professionista newyorkese di fama internazionale.

This book provides an eclectic and compound scenario, contrasting twenty-nine design projects of stores and boutiques, all created in the United States beginning in the 90's. These commercial environments have been selected to reflect a wide variety of stores: from trendy to more traditional, from spaces intended to appeal to a wider public to a unique selection of new and exclusive boutiques. At times comparable to art galleries, their interesting layouts offer a rich and stimulating survey of commercial architecture made in the USA. Each project has been photographed by Paul Warchol, a professional New Yorker of international fame and repute.

1999, 230 x 297, 240 pp., 218 ill. col. + 63 b/n, testo inglese/italiano.
€ 93,40 / L. 180.000 (rilegato/hardback)   ISBN 88-7685-105-4

7

EDIZIONI L'ARCHIVOLTO - via marsala 3 20121 milano - tel 0039.02.29010444 29010424 - fax 0039.02.29001942 - archivolto@homegate.it

Fotolito: San Patrignano - Rimini

Stampa: Euroteam - Nuvolera (BS)

Legatura: Zanardi Editoriale - Padova